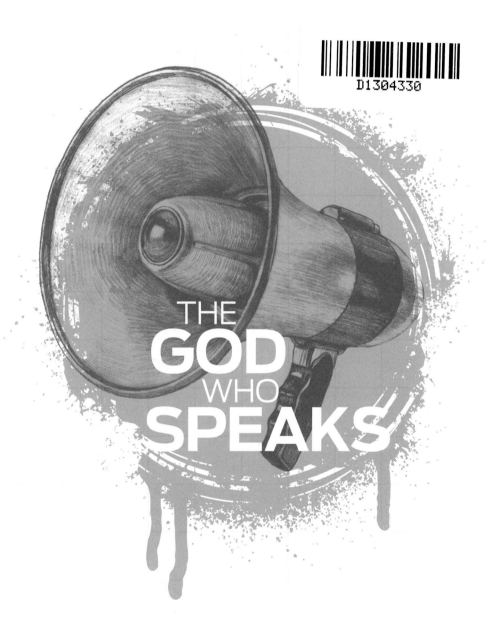

THE
GOD
WHO
SPEAKS

THE
GOSPEL
PROJECT
FOR STUDENTS

Ed Stetzer General Editor **Trevin Wax** Managing Editor

ISBN: 978-1-4158-7641-1
Item: 005541357
Dewey Decimal Classification Number: 230
Subject Heading: REVELATION \ GOD \ DOCTRINAL THEOLOGY

We believe that the Bible has God for its author; salvation for its end; and truth,
without any mixture of error, for its matter and that all Scripture is totally true and trustworthy.
To review LifeWay's doctrinal guideline, please visit *www.lifeway.com/doctrinalguideline.*

To order additional copies of this resource, write to
LifeWay Church Resources; One LifeWay Plaza; Nashville, TN 37234-0113;
phone toll free (800) 458-2772; fax (615) 251-5933;
e-mail *orderentry@lifeway.com*; order online at *www.lifeway.com*
or visit the LifeWay Christian Store serving you.

Printed in the United States of America.
Student Ministry Publishing
LifeWay Church Resources
One LifeWay Plaza
Nashville, Tennessee 37234-0144

TABLE OF CONTENTS

WRITERS

PART 1: THE GOD WHO SPEAKS

Trevin Wax is managing editor for *The Gospel Project* and the author of *Counterfeit Gospels* (Moody) and *Holy Subversion* (Crossway). He has served in pastoral roles in churches in the United States and Romania. He and his wife, Corina, reside in Middle Tennessee with their two children.

Jared Wilson is pastor of Middletown Springs Community Church and the author of *Gospel Wakefulness* (Crossway), *Seven Daily Sins*, and *Abide* (both LifeWay's Threads). He and his wife, Becky, reside in Vermont with their two children.

PART 2: OUR FALLEN RESPONSE TO GOD'S WORD

George Robinson is assistant professor of evangelism and missions at Southeastern Baptist Theological Seminary and the author of *Striking the Match*. He has served as a church planter in Pakistan and as a director for church planting equipping in numerous countries. He and his wife, Catherine, reside in Wake Forest, NC, with their three children.

PART 3: CHRIST'S PERFECT RESPONSE TO GOD'S WORD

Juan Sanchez is pastor of High Pointe Baptist Church in Austin, TX, where he lives with his wife, Jeanine, and their five daughters. Juan has served local churches in Florida, Georgia, and Indiana.

PART 4: OUR REDEEMED RESPONSE TO GOD'S WORD

Christian George earned his PhD from the University of St. Andrews in Scotland, where he studied his favorite Baptist hero, Charles Spurgeon. He is the author of *Sex, Sushi, & Salvation*, *Godology*, and *Sacred Travels* and currently serves as assistant professor of biblical and theological studies at Oklahoma Baptist University. Christian enjoys preaching, teaching, leading youth camps, and challenging his students to ping-pong tournaments. You can visit him online at *www.restlesspilgrim.com*.

Some people see the Bible as a collection of stories with morals for life application. But it is so much more. Sure, the Bible has some stories in it, but it is also full of poetry, history, codes of law and civilization, songs, prophecy, letters—even a love letter. When you tie it all together, something remarkable happens. A story is revealed. One story. The story of redemption through Jesus.

This is *The Gospel Project*.

When we begin to see the Bible as the story of redemption through Jesus Christ, God's plan to rescue the world from sin and death, our perspective changes. We no longer look primarily for what the Bible says about us but instead see what it tells us about God and what He has done. After all, it is the gospel that saves us, and when we encounter Jesus in the pages of Scripture, the gospel works on us, transforming us into His image.

We become God's gospel project.

The Gospel Project Core Values:

Deep, but not Dry.

We believe it's best to expect a lot out of those who attend a small group. We don't need to go only as deep as the least knowledgeable person in the group. We may have to "cut up the meat" for new believers and make sure the truth is accessible, but the important thing is that everyone has been fed and is sufficiently nourished.

Christ-Centered.

God is the primary Actor in the grand narrative of Scripture, and the gospel of Jesus Christ is the climax of this story. We approach the Old Testament as Jesus did on the road to Emmaus: all the Scriptures testify to Him. We approach New Testament ethics and commands as implications that flow from the gospel—Christ crucified and raised.

Story-Focused.

Being Christ-centered naturally brings our focus to the overarching story that the Bible tells in four parts: Creation / Fall / Redemption / Restoration. This helps us connect the dots, think as Christians formed by the great story that tells the truth about our world, and provides a hope-filled outlook on our world because of the future God has promised.

Mission-Driven.

Telling the story of the Bible is impossible without leading to mission, as the gospel reveals the heart of our missionary God and His desire to save people of every tribe, tongue, and nation. Keeping a focus on how the gospel leads us to mission is a crucial aspect of how we apply the Bible to our lives.

PART 1

THE GOD WHO SPEAKS

God speaks. And this is grace. He doesn't have to, and we would never be able to know Him otherwise. Yet God reveals Himself to His creation both through His creation and through His Word. These testify to who He is, and they point us to the Living Word—Jesus, the full revelation of God to man.

Voices from Church History

"When you come to knowing God, the initiative lies on His side. If He does not show Himself, nothing you can do will enable you to find Him." [1]

–C. S. Lewis (1898-1963)

CHAPTER 1

THE GOD WHO SPEAKS

The God Who Reveals Himself Through Creation

Voices from the Church

"The God of the Bible in the very first chapter is not some abstract 'unmoved mover,' some spirit impossible to define, some ground of all beings, some mystical experience. He has personality and dares to disclose himself in words that human beings understand. Right through the whole Bible, that picture of God constantly recurs. However great or transcendent he is, he is a talking God." [2]

–*D. A. Carson*

Voices from Church History

"You called and cried out loud and shattered my deafness. You were radiant and resplendent, you put to flight my blindness. You were fragrant, and I drew in my breath and now pant after you. I tasted you, and I feel but hunger and thirst for you. You touched me, and I am set on fire to attain the peace which is yours." [3]

–*Augustine (354-430)*

HE HAS AUTHORITY

Gen. 1:1-3 *In the beginning God created the heavens and the earth. Now the earth was formless and empty, darkness covered the surface of the watery depths, and the Spirit of God was hovering over the surface of the waters. Then God said, "Let there be light," and there was light.*

IMAGINE YOUR FAVORITE HANGOUT, LIKE a local pizza parlor or burger joint. Think about all the details that go into making it the place you know and love: music played, decoration, closing time, employees, cost of menu items, type of soda, items on the menu, etc. The list could go on and on and on.

Who has the final say in all of these many decisions? The owner of the restaurant. He or she has the final authority over all aspects of the place because he or she either built or purchased it. As the creator and sustainer of that establishment, they get to be the one who ultimately decides what this week's special is and who will be working which shifts. Everything that happens in their restaurant is subject to their authority. As the customer, can you really complain about the decorations or menu items? You can choose not to eat there, but you can't really complain because the restaurant isn't yours.

Let's now project this concept on a global level. Who has ultimate authority over the entire world? That would be God, the creator and sustainer of the entire universe. The Bible clearly states that God created the heavens and the earth. He created all the light we see simply by saying, "Let there be light." He created the sun, the moon, the stars, the oceans, the continents, the plants, the animals, and all of mankind simply by speaking them into existence. The same power used for speaking the entire universe into existence is now used to shape the universe for His purposes. As the creator and sustainer of the world, the God who speaks has the ultimate authority.

PAUSE AND REFLECT

▷ Why is it important to realize God's authority?

▷ What impact does God's authority have in your life?

▷ Do you find yourself disagreeing with what God has chosen or allowed to happen? Rather than disagreeing, what would be a better response?

THE CURTAIN IS OPEN

Ex. 3:2-6 *Then the Angel of the Lord appeared to him in a flame of fire within a bush. As Moses looked, he saw that the bush was on fire but was not consumed. So Moses thought: I must go over and look at this remarkable sight. Why isn't the bush burning up? When the Lord saw that he had gone over to look, God called out to him from the bush, "Moses, Moses!" "Here I am," he answered. "Do not come closer," He said. "Take your sandals off your feet, for the place where you are standing is holy ground." Then He continued, "I am the God of your father, the God of Abraham, the God of Isaac, and the God of Jacob." Moses hid his face because he was afraid to look at God.*

ONE OF THE FINAL SCENES in the classic movie The Wizard of Oz finds Dorothy, the Tin Man, the Lion, and the Scarecrow bringing the broom from the Wicked Witch of the West to the great and powerful Wizard of Oz. They are treated to a huge spectacle of smoke and fire. During this grand display, Toto wanders off and discovers a great truth: the Wizard of Oz is not a powerful person, but rather a tiny old man speaking into a microphone and pulling levers and buttons. Instead of being all-powerful, he was in fact powerless and hidden, afraid people would learn the truth.

This is the exact opposite of how God works. Rather than hiding behind a curtain, He has made Himself fully known. He is the creator of the universe, and He wants people to know who He is in a personal way.

The story of Moses and the burning bush is just one of many instances we see of God revealing Himself to His people. The Bible is full of other examples. These examples start in the book of Genesis as He created the heavens and the earth, and continue all the way through the book of Revelation as the Bible says that "the grace of the Lord Jesus be with all the saints" (Rev. 22:21). Because of His immense love for us, God mercifully reveals Himself to all of His creation.

PAUSE AND REFLECT

▷ **Why did the Wizard of Oz not want to be revealed?**

▷ **Why does God continuously reveal Himself?**

▷ **In what ways has God revealed Himself in your life?**

RESPONDING TO HIS BLESSING

Gen. 1:27-30 *So God created man in His own image; He created him in the image of God; He created them male and female. God blessed them, and God said to them, "Be fruitful, multiply, fill the earth, and subdue it. Rule the fish of the sea, the birds of the sky, and every creature that crawls on the earth." God also said, "Look, I have given you every seed-bearing plant on the surface of the entire earth, and every tree whose fruit contains seed. This food will be for you, for all the wildlife of the earth, for every bird of the sky, and for every creature that crawls on the earth—everything having the breath of life in it. I have given every green plant for food." And it was so.*

BAD NEWS: YOU JUST LOST YOUR IPHONE and with it your ability to communicate and survive. The following two scenarios are ways you may replace it.

Scenario 1: You know it is going to cost you something so you approach your parents with a proposal. You explain you will take on several household chores, including all yardwork, for the summer. In exchange for this work, you will earn the required money to pay for your lifeline to the outside world—your iPhone.

Scenario 2: Your dad found you staring out to space and eventually realized your helpless situation. Being a loving father, he stops by the store, picks up a brand new phone, and gives it to you that evening. Overwhelmed by love and gratitude, you decide to step up and take on more chores around the house. You even volunteer to paint the fence that desperately needs it and you want to continually show your love and gratitude so you joyfully mow the lawn each week without being asked.

Notice that in both situations, the end result is the same: you get a new iPhone, the fence gets painted, and the yard gets mowed. But the manner in which the end came about is completely different. The second scenario is similar to how things work with God. There is nothing we can ever do to earn His favor. But he loves and cares for us so much that the Bible says that He blesses us (Gen. 1:28). It was even more evident when He sent His only son to die on our behalf, so that we may have everlasting life (John 3:16). The point is, God does not give us tasks in order to earn His blessings. He gives us His blessings, which in turn ought to motive us to worship and obey Him!

PAUSE AND REFLECT

▷ Why doesn't God act in a manner similar to scenario 1?

▷ Why do so many people think God works like the father in scenario 1?

▷ How does seeing scenario 2 affect your thoughts about God and His commands?

THE GOD WHO SPEAKS

The God who speaks has authority, is merciful and gives us tasks.

GOD SPEAKS. From the beginning of time and in the pages of Scripture, God reveals Himself as a God who speaks. His speech is a demonstration of His power, grace, and authority. Because of this truth, there is nothing more important in life than hearing from God and obeying His voice.

Helen Keller was only 19 months old when a childhood illness left her deaf and blind, a prisoner to a world of incomprehensible sensations and inexpressible thoughts. "Have you ever been at sea in a dense fog, when it seemed as if a tangible white darkness shut you in?" she would later write. "'Light! Give me light!' was the wordless cry of my soul."

Years later, Helen Keller's parents hired a teacher, Anne Sullivan, who sought to break into the 6-year-old's world of silent darkness. Sullivan's breakthrough came when she taught Helen how to sign the word "water." Helen described the moment she first realized that her teacher was communicating with her:

> Some one was drawing water and my teacher placed my hand under the spout. As the cool stream gushed over one hand she spelled into the other the word water, first slowly, then rapidly. I stood still, my whole attention fixed upon the motions of her fingers. Suddenly I felt a misty consciousness as of something forgotten—a thrill of returning thought; and somehow the mystery of language was revealed to me. I knew then that "w-a-t-e-r" meant the wonderful cool something that was flowing over my hand. That living word awakened my soul, gave it light, hope, joy, set it free! There were barriers still, it is true, but barriers that could in time be swept away.2

The story of Helen Keller reminds us of the power of communication. In our wired world of iPhones and iPads, Facebook and Skype, we take for granted the ease of communication. We've grown accustomed to receiving a constant stream of information. The privilege of being personally addressed is overshadowed by the commonness of constant communication with family and friends.

Communication is common in the way that breathing and sleeping are common. Communicating is an important aspect of human existence, so much so that we consider it to be particularly harrowing to suffer from a disease that takes away a person's ability to communicate, especially when the mind is left intact.

Some people view human interaction as so vital to human flourishing that they protest the practice of placing prisoners in solitary confinement for an extended period of time. Opponents of solitary confinement believe complete solitude destroys the person's mental and relational capacities.

Regardless of one's view of the legitimacy of solitary confinement, it's fascinating that this kind of debate would even take place. The discussion itself demonstrates the importance of verbal interaction for human flourishing. We are relational beings. We were made for words—for hearing and for speaking.

No wonder the first chapter of the Bible focuses on the God who speaks. The first inspired words God spoke to us in the Bible are about Him speaking! This emphasis that God placed on communication should remind us of our need to hear from God. Without God choosing to reveal Himself to us, we are like Helen Keller—deaf and blind to the reality of the world we live in. Without God's revelation, we are unaware of His expectations for us and of His provision for salvation.

In upcoming chapters, we will examine the ways God reveals Himself. Theologians have divided the methods of God's revelation into two categories: **general revelation** and **special revelation**. General revelation refers to that which comes to all people everywhere (through creation, for example), whereas special revelation refers to that which is available to specific people at specific times and in specific places (through God's covenant with Israel or the sacred Scriptures). We will look at these categories in more detail in future chapters. For now, we will ponder the truth that God makes Himself known.

In this chapter, we will look at three truths that flow from the reality of God as Speaker. The goal of our lesson is to appreciate the goodness of God as seen in His revelation to us and then to spread the news that He has spoken by aligning our lives with His will and telling others of His grace.

THE GOD WHO SPEAKS...

▶ HAS AUTHORITY (GEN. 1:1-3).

Let's begin by looking at the first verses of the Bible, Genesis 1:1-3.

¹In the beginning God created the heavens and the earth. ²Now the earth was formless and empty, darkness covered the surface of the watery depths, and the Spirit of God was hovering over the surface of the waters. ³Then God said, "Let there be light," and there was light.

Notice the power of God's word in this passage. There was nothing but nothingness until God made His intentions known. With just two words spoken by God, light came into existence. God created by speaking. And the result of His speaking demonstrates how powerful His speech is.

Words change things. When a pastor stands next to a gushing groom and a beaming bride and says, "I now pronounce you husband and wife," their status changes. They become united before God and God's people. They are ushered into the union of holy matrimony. The spoken word changed them forever because it was spoken with authority.

But words have no authority in themselves. Words are only powerful when spoken by someone with power.

The reality TV show "*The Apprentice*" is a 13-week-long job interview where participants compete for the opportunity to become an apprentice to billionaire Donald Trump. At the end of each episode, Donald takes into consideration the performance of each team and each individual. Then with dramatic flair, he looks one of the candidates in the eye and says, "You're fired." End of discussion. Once these words are uttered, the room falls silent, and the candidate leaves the room. In every episode, "You're fired" changes the dynamic of the show—not because there is anything authoritative in these words, but because Donald Trump has the authority to make the decision.

If the words of a man who owns millions of dollars worth of property are powerful, how much more powerful are the words of God who owns everything in the universe!

Responding to the powerful nature of God's speech, the psalmist praised God for His creative authority: "Praise Him, sun and moon; praise Him, all you shining stars. Praise Him, highest heavens, and you waters above the heavens. Let them praise the name of Yahweh, for He commanded, and they were created" (Ps. 148:3-5). Notice the progression: God commanded, and the universe was created.

The power of God exercised through His word elicited this reaction from the writer of Hebrews: "For the word of God is living and effective and sharper than any double-edged sword, penetrating as far as the separation of soul and spirit, joints and marrow. It is able to judge the ideas and thoughts of the heart" (Heb. 4:12).

Words matter. Words carry weight. And the weightiest words are those uttered by the most glorious (the weightiest) Being in the universe. His words matter because of who He is.

The truth that God speaks is what separates Him from all idols. In the Old Testament, we see frequent showdowns between the true God of Israel and the false gods of pagan peoples. Whether it be the plagues God sent on Egypt (corresponding with the Egyptian gods; Ex. 7–12) or Elijah calling down fire on Mount Carmel (after the prophets of Baal cried out in vain; 1 Kings 18), the writers of the Bible delight in showing the power of God over idolatry. In Psalm 115:3-5, we read: "Our God is in heaven and does whatever He pleases. Their idols are silver and gold, made by human hands. They have mouths but cannot speak, eyes, but cannot see." The contrast is clear. God is Spirit. He has no physical mouth, and yet He speaks. The idols, on the other hand, are physical. They have mouths but are silent. God alone has authority. God is the God who speaks.

▶ IS MERCIFUL (EX. 3:2-6).

In Exodus 3:2-6, we are given a glimpse of how God revealed Himself to Moses in the form of a burning bush.

²Then the angel of the LORD appeared to him in a flame of fire within a bush. As Moses looked, he saw that the bush was on fire but was not consumed. ³So Moses thought: I must go over and look at this remarkable sight. Why isn't the bush burning up? ⁴When the LORD saw that he had gone over to look, God called out to him from the bush, "Moses, Moses!"

"Here I am," he answered.

⁵"Do not come closer," He said. "Remove the sandals from your feet, for the place where you are standing is holy ground." ⁶Then He continued, "I am the God of your father, the God of Abraham, the God of Isaac, and the God of Jacob." Moses hid his face because he was afraid to look at God.

This account shows us that mercy is at the heart of God's revelation to us. Notice who initiated the conversation. God is the One who came to Moses. He mercifully revealed Himself and then identified Himself as the God of Moses' forefathers.

Humans have no right to demand an audience with God. God is not accountable to us; we are accountable to Him. God would have been fully just and righteous to create this world and leave it to natural processes, never to intervene, never to communicate with His human creatures, and never to involve Himself with our human plight. There is nothing about our existence that forces God to be a God who reveals Himself. And yet God speaks. The very fact that we are created is a result of God's grace.

God was under no obligation to speak the world into existence. God does not need creation, as if He were lonely and longing to be praised. No, the God of the Bible is perfect in His Three-in-One nature. The Father overflows with love for His Son through the Holy Spirit. God's grace is the source of our creation. He created us to fellowship with Him, to join in the love song the three Persons of the Trinity sing to one another. Out of grace—not necessity—God has created this world. He has spoken, and therefore, we exist.

It is also an act of grace that God would reveal Himself to us personally. God was under no obligation to pull back the curtain and let us see aspects of His character and evidences of His power. He could have spoken the world into existence and then never spoken again, leaving us in ignorance about our Creator and our purpose.

In fact, some people hold to a worldview that imagines this very scenario. (And some Christians who don't believe this way still live this way!) Deism teaches that God created the world, much like a clockmaker puts together a clock. But then the Deist god no longer intervenes in our affairs. Deists believe that God cares very little about what happens in this world. He lets the clock begin to tick, and then he steps back and becomes uninvolved.

The Deist view of God is certainly plausible. But is it true? Not according to the Bible. Scripture is God's revealed truth to us, and according to this revelation, God has revealed Himself personally. His revelation is an act of mercy and grace.

In Deuteronomy 4:33, Moses reminded the Israelites of the great privilege they had received in hearing the voice of God. He asked, "Has a people heard God's voice speaking from the fire as you have, and lived?" The rhetorical effect of Moses' question demonstrates the mercy that comes from hearing God speak. The fact that God would choose to reveal Himself, and to do so in such a way as to allow us to live, is an act of mercy.

Here we see the good news of the gospel! The gospel is the story of a God who issues a call to helpless sinners. In our blindness and deafness, we are imprisoned by our own sinfulness. We cannot see the goodness of God until He gives us new eyes. We cannot hear the voice of God until He opens our ears. Like Helen Keller, we struggle to make sense of the world around us—why we are here and where we are going.

But God—out of sheer grace—chose to enter our world of darkness through the Person of Jesus Christ. John 1 says, "In the beginning was the Word, and the Word was with God, and the Word was God" (v. 1). And then, "The Word became flesh and took up residence among us" (v. 14). Jesus is God's Word to us, breaking through our dark, silent prison and saying, "Let there be light!" ("Life was in Him, and that life was the light of men. That light shines in the darkness, yet the darkness did not overcome it" [vv. 4-5].) In His perfect life and sacrificial death, Jesus revealed God to us. He showed us God's character. He demonstrated the love at the heart of the Father's authority.

God created us out of mercy. He has spoken to us out of mercy. He became one of us out of His mercy. And He calls us to Himself out of His mercy. Just as Anne Sullivan broke through to Helen, the Holy Spirit opens the eyes of our heart so we can see His goodness and His glory and respond with gratitude.

Thinking about "the God who speaks" is not merely an intellectual exercise. Revelation is more than a doctrine about the inspiration of the Scriptures. It is more than a doctrine about the beauty of God's creation. Revelation is at the very heart of what God has done on our behalf to bring Himself glory. As New Testament scholar Klyne Snodgrass has said, "Revelation does not merely bring the gospel: the gospel is revelation."[8]

▶ ## GIVES US TASKS (GEN 1:27-30).

If it is true that God has spoken, then there is nothing greater we can do than listen to what our Creator has said.

Once we recognize the authority of the God who speaks and the mercy from which He speaks, we are then responsible to lovingly and willingly obey God's commands. The command has been issued. What will our response be?

In Genesis 1:27-30, God told the first humans, Adam and Eve, what He expected of them.

[27] So God created man in His own image; He created him in the image of God; He created them male and female. [28] God blessed them, and God said to them, "Be fruitful, multiply, fill the earth, and subdue it. Rule the fish of the sea, the birds of the sky, and every creature that crawls on the earth." [29] God also said, "Look, I have given you every seed-bearing plant on the surface of the entire earth and every tree whose fruit contains seed. This food will be for you, [30] for all the wildlife of the earth, for every bird of the sky, and for every creature that crawls on the earth—everything having the breath of life in it. I have given every green plant for food." And it was so.

Notice the progression again: God created (authority); then He blessed (mercy). Finally, He gave tasks. Out of His authority, God created Adam and Eve. Out of His mercy, He blessed them. Then God's mercy led to His tasking Adam and Eve with cultivating His good creation.

Too many times we get the order backwards. We begin with the tasks of the Christian life and seek to receive God's blessing as a result of our obedience. But the gospel turns these expectations upside down. God first blesses His children. Only then does He task them with ruling wisely over the earth.

This pattern is seen in other places in Scripture as well. God first delivered the children of Israel from their slavery in Egypt. Then He gave them the law on Mount Sinai. In the New Testament, Christ died for our sins and rose again to new life, saving us from our sins. Then He reminded us of His authority as He commissioned us to take the gospel to all nations.

When we begin with the task rather than the blessing, we cut ourselves off from the very power that is necessary to fulfill the tasks God has given us. The blessing of the gospel—the gift of undeserved grace—should motivate and drive our obedience. As we embrace the gospel, the gospel then empowers our love for God and for our neighbor.

When we begin with our obedience instead of God's blessing, we invert the gospel. We begin to think that we can somehow put God in our debt. If we only do enough good works, maybe God will bless us. This is humanity's futile attempt at keeping control. We'd rather think that God owes us. As long as we think someone owes us, we maintain a sense of control.

Grace—in contrast—is scary! When we come to understand that accomplishing our task is made possible only because of God's initial blessing of grace, then there is nothing God can't ask of us. There is nothing He owes us. We owe Him everything— our very lives.

▶ CONCLUSION

After Anne Sullivan was able to communicate with Helen Keller, she began to teach her how to communicate with others. Anne did not speak to Helen in order to become merely a companion to her. Anne saw Helen's potential for communication. Helen Keller became an author and activist in later years. The power of that initial moment of communication led to places no one would have imagined.

So it is with us. God does not speak to us so that we might keep Him company or that we might merely be friends. He speaks to us and lavishes the grace of His salvation upon us so that we might then get to work accomplishing all that He has called us to do. The God who speaks is the God who gives tasks. God communicates His commands, and then He breathes His Spirit into our hearts, enabling us to learn, live, and love.

QUESTIONS

1. Why do you think God designed humans with an innate need to communicate? What does this design communicate about the nature and desire of God?

2. How does the impact of a word of encouragement or criticism change depending upon the person who says it?

3. List people whose words carry meaning both culturally and to you personally.

4. How does our belief that God has spoken affect our view of Scripture? The world we live in? Our day-to-day behavior?

5. If you were to hold to a Deist view of God's revelation, how would that affect your life? How would it affect your view of the Bible?

6. What do we learn about God through the fact that He has revealed Himself to us and desires a relationship with us?

7. Why do you think it is important that we understand this progression? What might happen when we seek to understand the task apart from God's blessing?

CHAPTER 2
GOD IS NOT HIDING
The God Who Reveals Himself Through Creation

Voices from the Church

"The created realm (creation) is a spectacular theater that serves as the cosmic matrix in which God's saving and judging glory can be revealed. God's glory is so grand that no less a stage than the universe—all that is or was and will be, across space and through time—is necessary for the unfolding of this all-encompassing drama." [1]

—James M. Hamilton Jr.

Voices from Church History

"The voices of visible creation…are equally clear to everyone…giving everyone the one message, that they were made by someone and do not exist of themselves." [2]

—Diodore of Tarsus (ca. A.D. 380)

THE SIGNS ARE EVERYWHERE

Ps. 19:1-6 *The heavens declare the glory of God, and the sky proclaims the work of His hands. Day after day they pour out speech; night after night they communicate knowledge. There is no speech; there are no words; their voice is not heard. Their message has gone out to all the earth, and their words to the ends of the inhabited world. In the heavens He has pitched a tent for the sun. It is like a groom coming from the bridal chamber; it rejoices like an athlete running a course. It rises from one end of the heavens and circles to their other end; nothing is hidden from its heat.*

"I HAVE TO SEE IT to believe it." Have you ever said those words? Did you really mean them? For example, have you ever seen a Dish Network satellite orbiting our earth? Do you have to see it to believe that it's there? Or can you trust that it's out there because you've watched TV at someone's house that has a dish and a receiver?

No sane person would question the existence of Dish Network satellites orbiting our earth, even though they can't see the physical satellite. Instead, they see the results of the satellite, which are the television programs they watch. No one believes in the existence of satellites because they actually see the satellites. They believe in satellites because the video image points back to the existence of the satellite.

Think about that idea for a minute. We believe in satellites not because we can see them directly, but because there is overwhelming evidence pointing to their existence. We can use this same line of reasoning when we think about God. Though we don't see Him face-to-face, we see a multitude of things in creation that point us to the fact that He exists. In this short passage above, we see two of these many pointers. The amazing contents of the skies, including the sun, the stars, the moon, the clouds, the atmosphere, and everything else up there point to the glory of God. Further, the separating of days and nights and the components of each of these further point to God. In essence, all of creation points us toward the reality of our God and Creator.

PAUSE AND REFLECT

▷ What are some other things that we can't see directly, but have results to point back to their existence? (i.e. gravity, wireless Internet, cell phone coverage, etc.)

▷ What evidences of God's existence do you see?

▷ Why do so many people have to "see" something in order to believe it?

WITHOUT EXCUSE

Rom. 1:20 *From the creation of the world His invisible attributes, that is, His eternal power and divine nature, have been clearly seen, being understood through what He has made. As a result, people are without excuse.*

IMAGINE YOU'RE A REPORTER FOR your school newspaper and your school has agreed to host a neutral-site football game. That is, two teams that you know nothing about are going to be playing on your school's field. You are given the assignment of covering the game for the paper.

As you arrive to the game and make your way through the stands to the press box, you see multiple things that give clues as to people's roles and responsibilities: You notice a woman who is wearing a big button containing the photo of number 87 and quickly discern that she is a proud parent. You see a man standing on the field wearing a black and white striped shirt, and know immediately he is there to referee the game. A man wearing a headset is obviously the coach. A group in uniform carrying instruments plays in the band. The list goes on and on.

Even though you know nothing about either school, within seconds you can discern parents, coaches, players, band members, cheerleaders, referees and more by looking out and seeing their distinguishing characteristics. You can know important qualities about these people simply by noticing key traits they posses.

In a similar manner, we can know much about God by looking at His creation. None of those individuals tries to hide his role in the football game, and God does not try to hide His role in the creation of the world. Beaches, mountains, forests, deserts, stars, sunrises, sunsets, rainstorms, and everything else we encounter in this world point us to the reality of who God is. Paul says that when we stop and really think about all the amazing things we see in this world, we cannot help but be confronted with the reality of a powerful and creative God!

PAUSE AND REFLECT

▷ What are some things we can learn about God by simply looking at the world around us?

▷ What are some things that we can't learn about God simply by looking at the world around us?

▷ Why can't we learn everything about God simply by looking at His creation?

NOT A SALESMAN

Acts 14:15-17 *"Men! Why are you doing these things? We are men also, with the same nature as you, and we are proclaiming good news to you, that you should turn from these worthless things to the living God, who made the heaven, the earth, the sea, and everything in them. In past generations He allowed all the nations to go their own way, although He did not leave Himself without a witness, since He did good: giving you rain from heaven and fruitful seasons, and satisfying your hearts with food and happiness."*

HAVE YOU EVER GONE INTO a department store to look for a new pair of jeans, and about five steps in encounter an overeager sales clerk asking you, "Is there anything I can help you with today?"

What causes us to be so hesitant to take them up on their offer? Is it because we genuinely don't want any help at all in the process of locating and purchasing jeans? Or is it because we're afraid that the sales clerk is more interested in padding her commission check than helping us find a pair that fits right?

This dilemma is a regular occurrence in our fallen world. We struggle to discern what others' intentions are. Do they really want to help with something, or do they simply want to receive something in return? Compare this feeling to when a friend offers to go along and help. It is easier to accept a friend's help because you generally know his motives.

What about the conversations and relationship you have with God? Do you ever wonder about His intentions for us? Do you ever question your intentions for Him?

God does not hide His intentions. He intends for us to worship and obey Him. He gave us the heavens, the earth, the sea, and everything in it to enjoy so that we might come to know Him. He gives us rain and food to sustain our physical needs. He gave His only Son to die on a cross to purchase our salvation. He has met and continues to meet every one of our needs so that we understand and accept the truth of the Gospel.

God's intentions are crystal clear. He created us, this world, and everything in it so that we might know Him and make Him known.

PAUSE AND REFLECT

▷ **Why do we so often question other people's intentions?**

▷ **Have you ever questioned God's intentions for your life? Why or why not?**

▷ **When you approach God in prayer, what are your intentions? Are you more sales person or friend?**

GOD IS NOT HIDING

Creation Teaches about His existence, his character and his motives.

IN THE 1998 FILM *The Truman Show,* Jim Carrey plays Truman Burbank, a generally cheerful insurance adjuster in a cozy island town whose days run like clockwork—until the day a stage light falls out of the heavens and crashes near his car. Though the news on the radio says an airplane has been shedding parts, Truman begins to develop a suspicious awareness that everything is not as it seems:

- A technical difficulty on his car stereo broadcasts his route.
- A homeless man calling his name on the street looks very much like the father he thought was dead.
- An elevator in an office building opens to reveal what looks like a backstage area.
- The traffic in Truman's neighborhood appears to run on a "loop."

As Truman begins paying attention to the world around him, he discovers little by little that he is the unwitting star of a reality television show. Everyone in his life is an actor, all the people he sees throughout the day are extras, and the island town he lives in is actually a gigantic set enclosed by a heavenly bubble and overseen by a television director with a God complex. As Truman begins looking back through his life and at the world around him, he realizes the clues to reality were there all along.

The Truman Show is just a movie, of course (although its human-in-a-bubble premise doesn't seem so strange in these days of strange reality television shows!), but it is nevertheless a good metaphor for how billions of people live their lives in this world every day. They wake up, go about their routines, and go to bed, only to start the ritual all over again. Sometimes they suspect the world around them is trying to tell them something about itself and what's outside of it, but they fail over and over again to put those clues together. They are like a person who finds a watch on the sidewalk and assumes it is the natural result of millions of years of sand, wind, and sun working together slowly forming a watch.

The movie is also a good metaphor for how billions of other people live their lives: seeing the signs in daily life (the sun's rising, the sea's swelling, the changing of the seasons, the clockwork of the solar system, the intricacies of DNA) as if they are falling lights and telltale radio broadcasts and peeks behind the stage. We find that watch on the sidewalk and know it didn't arrive there accidentally. It was dropped, it was owned, and before all that, it was made. The world is telling us something; we just know it! It's telling us something about itself, about us, and about what's behind it all. But what? What is it saying?

According to the Bible, the world around us is testifying to all within it that there is a Creator. Furthermore, the world around us is telling us what the Creator is like, and it is telling us something of His plans. We call this reality **general revelation** because it refers to the general way God reveals Himself to people everywhere.

CREATION TEACHES ABOUT...

▶ HIS EXISTENCE (PS. 19:1-6).

One of the most direct references to general revelation we find in the Scriptures is Psalm 19:1-6.

¹The heavens declare the glory of God,
and the sky proclaims the work of His hands.
²Day after day they pour out speech;
night after night they communicate knowledge.
³There is no speech; there are no words;
their voice is not heard.
⁴Their message has gone out to all the earth,
and their words to the ends of the world.
In the heavens He has pitched a tent for the sun.
⁵It is like a groom coming from the bridal chamber;
it rejoices like an athlete running a course.
⁶It rises from one end of the heavens
and circles to their other end;
nothing is hidden from its heat.

According to this passage, the created world is constantly saying something about its Creator—or more accurately, the Creator is constantly saying something about Himself through His created world. The picture we receive from the psalmist is of a world that acts as a loudspeaker, a stage, and an art gallery—all pointing to God's glory. The sky proclaims that all this work has a Designer's hands behind it.

Just like the presence of a watch on a sidewalk indicates a watchmaker, our finely tuned bodies living in this finely tuned world hanging in this finely tuned cosmos point to the logical existence of a Creator. Nobody looks at a Mercedes-Benz, for example, and assumes there was an explosion at a junkyard. According to the direct revelation of Psalm 19:1-6, the heavens (and the sky) are every day "pouring out speech" and every night "communicating knowledge" that God exists.

The sense we receive in verses 1-2 is of continual revelation. Creation never presses "pause" on its proclaiming that it is an effect, not a cause, and that it has an Originator. Verse 3 can be difficult to sort out, but the context of the passage gives us two most likely interpretations.

The first is that despite the nonstop speech and communication, some people simply ignore it as if it doesn't exist; the voice is not heard. Nevertheless, they cannot say they were not told, only that they did not listen. It is for a similar reason that Jesus, borrowing from Isaiah 6:9-10, says this in Matthew 13:15 of those people hardened to His message: "For this people's heart has grown callous; their ears are hard of hearing, and they have shut their eyes; otherwise they might see with their eyes and hear with their ears, understand with their hearts and turn back— and I would cure them."

The second possible interpretation of Psalm 19:3 is simply that David is noting the nature of general revelation, which is to say, it is not a speech that comes in an audible voice or literal words. The communication and knowledge are proclaimed, but not in the way direct, special revelation is. A watch tells us it has a watchmaker, but not in the same way as does shaking the watchmaker's hand and hearing his voice say, "I made that."

Both of these senses are true of Psalm 19:3. It is true that creation is proclaiming its Creator, but many either don't hear it or they hear it but reject it. It is also true that the way creation proclaims its Creator is not as direct as the way the Creator proclaims Himself.

In any event, verse 4 tells us that the "message has gone out to all the earth, and their words to the ends of the world." In other words, no place is absent general revelation. Nature's "music" points us to look for the Conductor. Nature's beauty points us to look for the Artist. The vastness of the Sahara Desert and the Arctic tundra and the mighty oceans, in making us feel small and vulnerable, point us to God, the strong Tower.

But the general revelation in the created order of the universe doesn't just tell us that there is a God; it tells us something about that God. To borrow a phrase from C. S. Lewis, general revelation doesn't merely tell us *a* God exists, it tells us *this* God exists.

Psalm 19:1 tells us "The heavens declare the glory of God," not merely the presence of God. The word "glory" has the sense of "weightiness" or "worth." God's glory is the sum impression of all that God is.

What we learn first about God from His general revelation is that God will not settle for being acknowledged. He wants to be known! So there is something about the heavens—their vastness, their beauty, their complexity, their power, their impression upon little ol' us—that tells us something about Him.

▶ HIS CHARACTER (ROM. 1:20).

Suppose you came home one day to find a package with this note attached: "These are the personal effects of your twin brother Joe, recently deceased." Once you got over the initial shock of discovering you had a twin brother you never knew about, you'd open the package and look at the contents, hoping they might tell you something about this brother.

If the package contained a leather jacket, a set of brass knuckles, and some cigarettes, that wouldn't tell you everything about your brother, but it would certainly give you a general impression, wouldn't it? And if the package contained instead a set of watercolor paints, a beret, and a tin of organic breath mints, that might give you an entirely different impression, wouldn't it? The package's existence would tell you that you had a brother, but the package's *contents* would tell you a bit about him.

In the same way, the created world tells us we have a God, and what we see in the created world tells us some general things about Him. By seeing the general revelation of "the heavens" and the rest of the world, we can get a sense of God's glory, the sum of His attributes.

In Romans 1:20, Paul writes:

²⁰For His invisible attributes, that is, His eternal power and divine nature, have been clearly seen since the creation of the world, being understood through what He has made. As a result, people are without excuse.

What Paul is getting at is that nobody can rightfully say, "I never heard the gospel message contained in the Bible, so I am not responsible for my own sin," because there is enough evidence of God's sovereign rule (over both people and their sin) in general revelation that nobody can say they weren't directed to seek Him out in special revelation.

Again, we should repeat that general revelation does not tell us all there is to know about God, nor can we hear the specific gospel message of salvation in the declarations of the heavens. Still, enough is communicated that "people are without excuse." Paul says the visible world reveals God's invisible attributes, namely, His "eternal power and divine nature."

God's "eternal power" can have two meanings. The first is that God's power is without end or limit. This is an affirmation of His omnipotence.

The other sense "eternal power" can have is that the power to sustain everything for all time belongs to God. In the first sense we are told what God's power is like; in the second sense we are told what God's power does. He upholds eternity.

How is this invisible attribute reflected in visible creation? We see God's eternal power revealed through the vastness of the cosmos and through the mighty forces at work in nature. The expanse of space or the unfathomable depths of the ocean ought to humble mankind. The same is true of an eruption of a volcano or the strength of a tsunami. These shows of power give us an otherworldly and overwhelming sense of being in the presence of the divine Being. As Matt Chandler has said, "Nobody stands at the base of the Rocky Mountains and says, 'Remember that time I benched 300 pounds in high school?'"

We see that God's power upholds eternity when we really begin to ponder the clocklike order of the universe. The planets are precisely aligned for earth's specialness. The conditions on earth are precisely balanced for life. The chemicals in human life are precisely proportioned for growth, intelligence, and creativity. Also, despite the destructive forces of tornadoes, hurricanes, earthquakes, lightning, tsunamis, floods, volcanic eruptions, and asteroids falling from the sky, this place keeps on keeping on. If we cannot see the sustaining power of God's providential care in creation's endurance, we likely will not see it in the pages of Scripture.

How is God's "divine nature" revealed through what we see? One of the clearest imprints is not just in the way we search for objects to worship but is right here inside, in the way we think and act. We read in Genesis 1:27: "So God created man in His own image; He created him in the image of God; He created them male and female."

Because we are creatures made in God's image, we have innate senses and compulsions that point to the reality of God's divine nature. Of course, we are not divine ourselves, and after the fall of mankind, the image of God in us is obscured and broken. Still, we can nevertheless see that mankind's generally innate sense of justice and fairness, compulsion to create, ability to express and experience love, and frequent appeals to conscience all point away from our being the evolved result of a random electric current in a primordial goop.

If you listen to children playing long enough, you will eventually hear the recurring cry, "That's not fair!" While we all have a moral compass that's skewed in the wiring due to sin, we still have an innate sense of right and wrong, just and unjust, fair and unfair. Apart from the Spirit's discipline, it is impossible for us to apply these impulses in selfless ways, but the presence of them to begin with indicates an ultimate right and an ultimate justice. Thanks to special revelation, we know that this is found in our perfectly holy and just God.

There is yet a third message we receive in general revelation. The visible world tells us that there is a God as well as something about what God is like, but the visible world still further tells something about God's plans.

▶ HIS MOTIVES (ACTS 14:15-17).

In Acts 14, Barnabas and Paul are in Lystra when a priest of Zeus begins to lead a crowd in making sacrifices to him. Barnabas and Paul, in dramatic fashion, interrupt the proceedings, tear their clothes, and proclaim:

15 "Men! Why are you doing these things? We are men also, with the same nature as you, and we are proclaiming good news to you, that you should turn from these worthless things to the living God, who made the heaven, the earth, the sea, and everything in them. 16 In past generations He allowed all the nations to go their own way, 17 although He did not leave Himself without a witness, since He did what is good by giving you rain from heaven and fruitful seasons and satisfying your hearts with food and happiness."

What did Barnabas and Paul want the people of Lystra to know? As the pagan demand for more sacrifices to a dead god continued, Barnabas and Paul desperately wanted these people to know the good news that Jesus has made the sacrifice to end all sacrifices, and He did so to honor the will of a Heavenly Father who had been far better to the unsaved people of Lystra than Zeus had been. The missionaries pointed to the evidence: "You have a witness that this is true!" they cried. "He has given you rain and harvest and good food and happiness."

In Romans 8:22, Paul writes, "For we know that the whole creation has been groaning together with labor pains until now." The image is that of the earth giving birth, but the focus is on the earth going through pain as it gives way to newness. What we look forward to is the return of Christ and the ushering in of the new heavens and the new earth (2 Pet. 3:13). The brokenness we see in "the whole creation," then, is signaling to us that (a) something is wrong and (b) there is something better.

Acts 14:17 and Romans 8:22 give us the imprint of the gospel story! Looking at the world around us, we recognize that this place is broken but there is pleasure to be had. This is the concept of "common grace," which we also see in Matthew 5:45: "For He causes His sun to rise on the evil and the good, and sends rain on the righteous and the unrighteous." The benevolent heart of God is made visible through common grace.

God intends for the happiness we experience in sports, relationships, and His other good gifts to point us back to Him. The gifts everyone enjoys in this life lead to the Giver. Yet not everyone has eyes to see. While we can't receive the gospel message in general revelation, we can certainly see its echoes.

▶ CONCLUSION

The Reformers thought of the world as a grand theater in which God showcases His glory. One thing we must say about this theater, of course, is that it is not itself the story but the stage for it. Like a good stage set, it tells us something of the story before the players even enter and begin reciting their lines. But it is the script that really reveals.

In *Mere Christianity,* C. S. Lewis tells of the time an old Air Force officer interrupted his talk on religion to say: "I'm a religious man too. I *know* there's a God. I've *felt* Him: out alone in the desert at night: the tremendous mystery. And that's just why I don't believe all your neat little dogmas and formulas about Him. To anyone who's met the real thing they all seem so petty and pedantic and unreal!"

Lewis goes on to honor the man's experience of "feeling God's presence" out in the wilderness of nature, but he denies that that sort of experience is sufficient. He writes: "You see, what happened to that man in the desert may have been real, and was certainly exciting, but nothing comes of it. It leads nowhere. There is nothing to do about it. In fact, that is just why a vague religion—all about feeling God in nature, and so on—is so attractive. It is all thrills and no work; like watching the waves from the beach. But you will not get to Newfoundland by studying the Atlantic that way, and you will not get eternal life by simply feeling the presence of God in flowers or music."[9]

QUESTIONS

1. What are some of the hints and clues we see in creation that point us to the existence of a Creator? Conversely, what are some of the aspects of creation that cause some people to believe that no Creator exists?

2. When you observe the world around you, what thoughts come to mind? Do you see beautiful scenery or His handiwork? When is the last time you really noticed His handiwork? Describe what you saw.

3. Think about the ways people attempt to guard themselves from God's revelation. What are some of the most common ways we try to hide from God's voice? What are some of the common ways we try to drown it out?

4. What is the difference between being acknowledged and being known?

5. What knowledge of God's character do we gain by looking at creation?

6. What does the complexity and variety of nature tell us about God?

7. If God is revealing Himself through creation and created things, what might the implications of this be on our own creativity?

8. Name some of God's attributes revealed in the Bible. How might some of these be communicated in the visible world? Where and how do we see them proclaimed in nature, including in general human experience?

9. What does the description of Paul and Barnabas' actions in Acts 14:11-18 tell us about evangelistic motives, demeanor, strategy, and message?

10. What are some other general revelation "signposts" we find in creation that illustrate the gospel of Jesus' life, death, and resurrection?

11. Why is it wrong to think that "experiencing God" in nature is enough?

12. How will the truth of general revelation help or otherwise affect your mission to be a witness to the gospel of Jesus?

CHAPTER 3
GOD IS NOT MUTE
The God Who Reveals Himself Through His Word

Voices from Church History

"The Word of God is always alive, fresh, and pertinent; it addresses itself to our present hour." [1]

–*W. A. Criswell (1909-2002)*

Voices from Church History

"Each sacred writer was by God specially formed, endowed, educated, providentially conditioned, and then supplied with knowledge naturally, supernaturally, or spiritually conveyed, so that he, and he alone, could, and freely would, produce his allotted part." [2]

–*Archibald A. Hodge and*
Benjamin B. Warfield (19th century)

HE INSPIRES

2 Tim. 3:16-17 *All Scripture is inspired by God and is profitable for teaching, for rebuking, for correcting, for training in righteousness, so that the man of God may be complete, equipped for every good work.*

THE BIBLE IS THE WORD of God. To use the theological word for it, it is an "inspired" book. That doesn't mean that the writers of the Bible fell into a trance and then woke up several hours later with pages in front of them. It means instead that God chose to use, as His instrument, these men, complete with their own personalities.

Think about it in terms of a text. If you want to be really particular and specific in what you communicate, you might use an emoticon. Or a different color. Or all capital letters. In the same way, God not only chose the words, He also chose the instruments He would use to communicate those words.

Have you ever wondered why there are four gospels? Wouldn't it be simpler if there was just one? But think about the differences in those gospels. Matthew was a former tax collector. He had a Jewish background. So His gospel includes these elements.

Mark appears to write from a Jewish perspective but to a gentile audience. Luke was a physician by trade. He had an organized and logical mind. His gospel displays that organization and logic. John started following Jesus when he was a teenager. His gospel has that mindset of imagination and creativity to it, complete with the flowery language.

Four different men. Four different perspectives on the same story. All inspired by one God. There is great hope for us in this fact. It means, among other things, that God has wired you, too, very specifically. He has given you talents and abilities, ingraining them into your very DNA. If God used these four men, along with the other writers of Scripture, according to their own personalities, then He's sure likely to use you, too. He's likely to use your creativity. Your love of sports or animals. Your physical makeup and being.

God can use you. He is, after all, the One who made you.

PAUSE AND REFLECT

▷ Have you ever wondered why you have the gifts and abilities you have?

▷ What ability do you secretly wish you had?

▷ How does knowing that God allowed men to write the Bible and used their uniqueness to accomplish His mission impact the way you look at how He has gifted you?

HE INSTRUCTS

Psalm 19:7-11 *The instruction of the LORD is perfect, renewing one's life; the testimony of the LORD is trustworthy, making the inexperienced wise. The precepts of the LORD are right, making the heart glad; the command of the LORD is radiant, making the eyes light up. The fear of the LORD is pure, enduring forever; the ordinances of the LORD are reliable and altogether righteous. They are more desirable than gold—than an abundance of pure gold; and sweeter than honey, which comes from the honeycomb. In addition, Your servant is warned by them; there is great reward in keeping them.*

"WHAT IS GOD'S WILL FOR my life?" It's a popular question that most every Christian (hopefully) asks at some point. Usually it's around a time of big decision—where to go to college, who to seriously date, what studies to pursue—something like that.

The question is a good one. It shows that we really want to do what God wants us to do; otherwise, we wouldn't really be asking the question. The truth is that for most everything, God has already revealed His will for our lives.

There are certain things you can do that you absolutely know are God's will for your life, because they're the same for every believer. These are things like:

- Study and memorize Scripture
- Avoid sexual immorality
- Pray on all occasions
- Seek to make disciples of all nations

No one has to ask about God's will in these matters; He's already revealed it. In fact, if most of us would seek to commit ourselves fully to the aspects of God's will that He has already revealed, then the other aspects of God's will might not be so mysterious to us.

Say, for example, you are trying to choose where to go to college. You know that it's God's will for your life to share the gospel and commit your life to bringing glory to Him in all contexts. The question then becomes "Where can I best live out what I know that God wants me to do?"

The only way we grow in this area is through reading, meditating on, and memorizing God's Word. This is how we learn God's will for our lives.

PAUSE AND REFLECT

▷ Do you find God's ways more desirable than gold or sweeter than honey?

▷ What areas of your life right now may be hindering you from finding His will for you?

▷ What prevents you from living out what you already know to be true?

HE'S ALWAYS BEEN THERE

Luke 24:25-27 *He said to them, "How unwise and slow you are to believe in your hearts all that the prophets have spoken! Didn't the Messiah have to suffer these things and enter into His glory?" Then beginning with Moses and all the Prophets, He interpreted for them the things concerning Himself in all the Scriptures.*

BIBLE STUDY WON'T CHANGE YOUR life. OK, that may be a bit of overstatement to get your attention, but just because you know the Bible doesn't mean the Word will bear fruit in your life. It is possible to know the Scriptures, read the Scriptures, revere the Scriptures, and study the Scriptures and miss the point entirely.

Way too often Bible study is more about us than Christ. We commonly begin with us at the center and bring God into our world to address our already-defined needs and problems. We look at the Bible as a book of divine instruction, a manual for succeeding in life, or a map for making sure we get to heaven when we die. Studying the Scripture like this will not result in life transformation. Why? Because it is missing something. Better put, it is missing Someone.

Bible study alone is not what transforms your life. Jesus transforms your life. It's possible to amass great amounts of biblical knowledge, to impress people with your mastery of Bible trivia, to creatively apply the Bible in ways that seem so down to earth and practical, to dot your theological I's and cross your exegetical T's — and still miss Jesus. Scary, isn't it?

The purpose of our Bible study is to know God and make Him known. The Bible unveils Jesus Christ as the focal point of human history. All creation exists by Him, through Him, to Him, and for Him. Our Bible study should exist for Him too. That's the only kind of Bible study that will change your life.

PAUSE AND REFLECT

▷ **Why is it important that all of the Bible is pointing to Christ?**

▷ **What is the difference in knowing things about Jesus and actually knowing Him?**

▷ **Which would you say best describes you: Knowing about Him or actually knowing Him?**

GOD IS NOT MUTE

Scripture is inspired by God, reveals his expectations, and glorifies Christ.

THE LAST CHAPTER CONSIDERED general revelation—the way in which God reveals Himself to us through His creation. Imagine you are walking along a sidewalk and discover a wristwatch on the ground. When you pick it up to examine it, would you deduce that it was the random result of an explosion in a metal and glass factory? Would you assume from its design and precision that it had come into being purely by accident, the fortuitous result of some minor cataclysm? Perhaps you know a little about science, and while some scientists argue that highly developed organization does result from disorganized material "naturally," you know that the second law of thermodynamics states that natural things actually are constantly breaking down. So that wristwatch could not have assembled itself out of dust, and if you left that wristwatch on the ground for a billion years, it would not turn into Big Ben, but to dirt. What do you assume then?

You assume the watch was made on purpose. Some outside, intelligent force used the means at its disposal to gather or manufacture the materials, to design the internal mechanism and the external display, and to put it all together so that—voila!—the watch was made. To the logical mind, the watch reveals the existence of a watchmaker.

As in the general revelation of God's glory in creation, the watch may reveal some things about its maker: that he has a keen eye, that he has an expert hand, and the like. These characteristics are clearly evident. They tell us things we ought to know about the maker's existence and his character. But all of the things the watch tells us about its maker have to be deduced. And they don't tell us some of the most critical things about the watchmaker—his name, for instance.

Facebook is a fantastic way of thinking about how general revelation differs from special revelation. General revelation is like our Facebook friends that we don't really know. They may be a friend of one of our friends but all we really know about them is what we find on their Facebook page. We may think we have a lot in common with them based on what we see. We may even think we know something about them, their personality, their character, or their talents. Unfortunately, while we may think we know something about them, we don't really know them. In order to really know them, we would need to meet them personally. Spend time with them, talk to them, live life with them. That is what real friends do. They move beyond knowing about each other and begin actually knowing each other.

God has revealed many things through creation, but His plan for redeeming creation can't be found in a beautiful sunset. Thankfully we have His actual words to guide us through Christ to a personal relationship with the Father. Through this relationship we can actually KNOW God, not just a few things about Him.

Scripture...

▶ **IS INSPIRED BY GOD (2 TIM. 3:16-17).**

Though the Bible has approximately 40 different authors, covers history to law, prophecy to poetry, and includes 66 books written over the span of 1,600 years, it has one Author who made every word sure and every truth proclaimed. Paul reminds Timothy of this vital truth in 2 Timothy 3:16-17:

16All Scripture is inspired by God and is profitable for teaching, for rebuking, for correcting, for training in righteousness, 17so that the man of God may be complete, equipped for every good work.

This short passage reveals to us a few things about itself and every other verse in the Bible. First, it tells us that every word of Scripture comes from God Himself, that they are "inspired" by the Holy Spirit. But what does this sort of inspiration mean?

That God inspired the Scriptures does not mean that men wrote the words of the Bible completely of their own devices merely as an act of honor to God. Certainly their work in writing the books of the Bible was an act of honor to God, but it was not *merely* that. So when we say God inspired men to write the Bible, we don't mean it in the same way that a guy may write a poem because he was inspired by a beautiful girl. The inspiration that the Holy Spirit provided in revealing the Word of God was direct, not indirect.

On the other hand, the inspiration that the Spirit provided in the revelation of the Word of God did not turn the human authors into writing robots. They weren't possessed—at least not in the sense of losing control over their own faculties. God used men to write the Bible, but He did so without overriding their personalities.

God may have used a variety of means to inspire the human authors of the Bible, but He ensured the final result was His own supreme authorship.

2 Timothy 3:16-17 also tells us something else. Because all Scripture is authored by God, all Scripture has authority over us. This is implicitly evident in the acknowledgment that through the Bible the sovereign God of the universe is declaring and commanding.

But it is explicitly evident in the way Paul tells Timothy that the Word of God contains all that we need to be "complete" and "equipped for every good work."

The words "complete" and "every" mean there is nothing necessary for us to know that the Bible lacks to show. And since the Bible's help for us in these areas is comprehensive and exclusive, it is therefore authoritative. We should neither need nor want to look outside of the Bible to find out what God deems as "need to know" knowledge.

In recent years, we've seen a number of books chronicling near-death experiences and visits to heaven and back. Depending on your perspective, these stories are really encouraging or dubious and discard-worthy.

But we can observe in the popularity of "visiting heaven books" a troubling sentiment about the Bible. Setting aside for the moment whether the stories in the book actually happened and the extra-biblical innovation some of them reveal (people who go to heaven get wings, according to some), it appears that for many Christians the book "proves" the truth of the Scriptures. "See?" many say. "The Bible is true after all! This person went to heaven and back." But we don't need people outside the Bible to tell us that. The words inside the Bible tell us that quite plainly. Similarly, the excitement generated by these books, as if they somehow authenticate the Christian worldview and the narrative of the gospel, can reveal a lack of confidence in the Bible itself, which is authenticated and authoritative all on its own. The Bible doesn't need our fantastic experiences to verify it. It is the very Word of God from the very breath of God.

One complication we often miss in the modern fantastic tales of heavenly adventure is that the hero tends to be the teller of the story. It is not always wrong to celebrate human achievement, of course, but as it pertains to spiritual things, it is clear that the hero of the Bible's story is not man but God Himself. God is the major Actor in the grand, biblical epic. Even the mightiest and cleverest of men in the Bible are revealed to be sinful, broken servants to our glorious God. And everything God reveals in the Bible is meant to amplify His own glory. This means that while the Bible is a message *for* us, it is ultimately a message *about* God. All that God does in the great history of redemption He does chiefly for His own renown.

▶ REVEALS HIS EXPECTATIONS (PS. 19:7-11).

In the general revelation of creation, we can discern God's existence and the shape of some of His attributes. These leave us without excuse in our responsibility to seek God and obey Him. But even though we see the imprint of the gospel in general revelation, we do not receive His specific word to us regarding what He expects from His relationship with us. In fact, while general revelation reveals there is a God to know, special revelation reveals that God *wants* to be known personally.

In our last chapter on general revelation, we surveyed Psalm 19:1-6 and discovered that "the heavens declare the glory of God," that creation reveals that God is speaking. Continuing on in verses 7-11, we see what David indicates God is actually saying in special revelation.

> *⁷The instruction of the LORD is perfect, renewing one's life;*
> *the testimony of the LORD is trustworthy, making the inexperienced wise.*
> *⁸The precepts of the LORD are right, making the heart glad;*
> *the command of the LORD is radiant, making the eyes light up.*
> *⁹The fear of the LORD is pure, enduring forever;*
> *the ordinances of the LORD are reliable and altogether righteous.*
> *¹⁰They are more desirable than gold—than an abundance of pure gold;*
> *and sweeter than honey, which comes from the honeycomb.*
> *¹¹In addition, Your servant is warned by them; there is great reward in keeping them.*

Just like any author wants to be interpreted correctly, God expects His people to desire His Word and to properly interpret it by putting into practice all He commands. In Psalm 19:7-11, David reminds us of what we learn in 2 Timothy 3:16-17, namely, that God's special revelation is perfect and trustworthy.

We do not worship the deist's god, who leaves clues about himself scattered about the universe but then goes hands-off and leaves us to our own deductive devices. No, we worship the God of Abraham, Isaac, and Jacob. We worship the God who interrupts us when we're trying to mind our own business, and He tells us His name, His plan, and His complete set of instructions on what to do with them. The great I AM is not content to be discerned; He wants to be known.

God does not want us to fumble around in the shadows, trying to figure out the meaning of life. He tells us where we stand in relation to Him (sinners deserving wrath), how we got there (through Adam's sin, which we both inherit and embrace), and best of all, how we get out of it into a right standing with Him (through Christ's sinlessness, culminating in His sacrificial death and glorious resurrection). Thanks be to God that He does not expect us to piece these expectations together solely through the changing of the seasons or the pervasive injustice in the world or the metamorphosis of a butterfly! He tells us straight out.

But David goes further. He not only speaks of the reality of God's expectations in His declarations, he speaks of the *quality* of these expectations. God's revelation is good for "renewing one's life" (v. 7), "making the heart glad" (v. 8), and "making the eyes light up." They are "more desirable than gold" and "sweeter than honey" (v. 10).

A popular allegory often used to illustrate how mankind "knows" things is Plato's cave. Plato reasoned that life for us is like living in a cave for one's whole life, mistaking the shadows on the wall cast by a fire as reality. We simply grasp at and scrutinize the forms of reality (the shadows), remaining largely blind to true reality (the fire and life outside the cave). This sounds somewhat similar to Paul's words in 1 Corinthians 13:12: "For now we see indistinctly, as in a mirror…" Without the special revelation of Scripture, then, we are like the "inexperienced" of Psalm 19:7, fumbling about in Plato's cave. We see the shadows in general revelation, which are proof enough of a greater reality. But thanks to God's special revelation, we are turned to the fire and our "eyes light up." We are moved from indistinct vision to the radiance of God's commandment, which ultimately reveals to us the Light of the world, Jesus Christ.

Many of us are not used to thinking of God's commandments—and Scripture in general—as "sweeter than honey," or something that is delicious. Even if we can reckon with the idea of loving God's law, we may have trouble figuring out how not to think of it in the context of a religious duty or a "chore chart" (something followed but not particularly enjoyed in my home!). But the Psalms speak of God's children delighting in God's law. How in the world do we get to that perspective?

▶ GLORIFIES CHRIST (LUKE 24:25-27).

The way we find God's commands delightful and His instruction tasty like honey is by moving beyond what God requires of us and seeing what He has accomplished Himself. As we learned before, God Himself is the Hero of God's story, and as it pertains to His desire to be known, He Himself bridges the communication gap we are unable to span ourselves. He does this first by speaking into the shadows of general revelation in the special revelation of Scripture. He does this savingly by speaking in the special revelation of Scripture the great announcement of the gospel of Jesus. The point of special revelation, then, is to reveal the gospel. God's written Word points to Jesus, the Living Word. Don't take my word for it, however. Listen to Jesus Himself:

25 He said to them, "How unwise and slow you are to believe in your hearts all that the prophets have spoken! 26 Didn't the Messiah have to suffer these things and enter into His glory?" 27 Then beginning with Moses and all the Prophets, He interpreted for them the things concerning Himself in all the Scriptures.

After Jesus was raised from the dead, He caught up with a couple of disciples making a trek to Emmaus. He sidled up alongside them and preached the greatest Christ-centered, expository sermon from the Old Testament ever preached in the history of the world.

"The point of all that," Jesus essentially said, pointing to the varied wonders of what we call the Old Testament, "is Me."

As Jesus claimed implicitly and explicitly throughout His earthly ministry that He is the true Messiah long awaited by the people of God, He was asserting Himself as the culmination of human history.

▶ READING THE SCRIPTURES WITH CHRIST AT THE CENTER

We can see the light of Christ in the shadow of the "first gospel" in one of the Bible's earliest stories, when God curses the serpent in Genesis 3:15. Here is a foreshadow of the saving cross of Christ, where Jesus' heel was simultaneously struck in crucifixion and He was victorious over sin and death, crushing the head of evil with His pierced feet.

We see the light of Christ in the shadow of the Old Testament's "last gospel," when Malachi 4 predicts the Day of the Lord. Who brings both wrath and redemption? Who is elsewhere referred to as the sun (Rev. 21:23)? Who is said to arrive on this Day of the Lord (Acts 2:17-24; 1 Thess. 5:1-10)? Who alone can do a supernatural work of reconciliation?

The answer is ever and always Jesus. His footprints are throughout the sand of the Old Testament. And the further light of the New Testament helps us see Him most clearly, from His incarnation to His glorification. All of the stories the Bible tells tell the unified story of how God glorifies Himself through the redemption of sinners who are made right with Him through the saving work of His Son, Jesus Christ.

None of this means that the Bible doesn't give us what we call "propositional truth." The Bible is not a story in the same way a novel is a story. It is a story in the sense that throughout all its genres and revelations, the overarching theme or message being communicated is that God saves sinners through the life, death, and resurrection of Jesus Christ.

Coming back to Psalm 19 and the delicious honey we find in God's commands, knowing the "big story" running through and connecting all the words of the Bible, we can see how we might move from duty to delight. When we receive the illumination of Jesus Christ, our eyes light up with the grace of God found in Him who is the radiance of the Father's glory (Heb. 1:3). When we receive Jesus as the Bread of life, we will taste and see that God is good. And when we are set free from our sins and the curse of the law's demands, we are finally free to obey God with joy and gratitude, delighting in His law rather than buckling under its weight.

Psalm 19:11 tells us there is "great reward" in keeping God's commands. We can't do that. But Jesus can and did. And there is great reward in Christ's righteousness for all who will repent of their sin, trust in His work, and thereby receive His goodness credited to their account.

▶ CONCLUSION

Through His Word, God specifies His intentions for humanity and His expectations of us. He shows us how the glory of Christ is the purpose of world history. We are to respond to God's special revelation by aligning ourselves with God's expressed will.

QUESTIONS

1. What does the truth that God chose not to override the personalities of the Bible's authors say about our own personalities? In what ways can God use our circumstances and personalities in our proclamation of His truth?

2. In what ways might Christians be tempted to supplement the Bible's authority with something else? How can we demonstrate our belief that the Bible is sufficient to guide our lives?

3. Do you agree with the statement "In all God does, His first aim is to glorify Himself"? Why or why not? What are some ways that God's glorifying Himself is a benefit to us?

4. In what ways can God's instructions make the heart glad? In what ways can God's commandments make our eyes light up? Are His ways sweeter than honey to you?

5. Reread Psalm 19:11. How is there great reward in keeping God's commandments? How does your answer to the above question relate to the truth that we are saved by faith, not by works (Eph. 2:8-9)?

6. Reflecting on Jesus' revelation to His traveling companions in Luke 24:25-27, what might have been some of "the things concerning Himself" He showed them from the Old Testament?

7. What part of your life is working counter to God's intentions?

8. Does God's voice have a presence in your life?

9. Are you instructed, rebuked, and corrected by the Word?

10. Is it possible to revere the Word and not read it?

11. How can you discipline yourself to spend unhurried time in God's Word

The God who speaks has authority, is merciful, and gives us tasks.

Creation Teaches about His existence, his character and his motives.

Scripture is inspired by God, reveals his expectations, and glorifies Christ.

PART 2

OUR FALLEN RESPONSE TO GOD'S WORD

God has graciously spoken. He has given us His clear expectations. But like our first parents, we view God's Word with suspicion and doubt, even though it is perfectly true, trustworthy, and authoritative—just like its Author. We question, belittle, and disobey the Word of the very One who created us. Dead in our sin, we cannot fix ourselves; we have fallen, and we need God's grace to lift us up.

Voices from Church History

"Remember what sin is: fundamental independence of God; the thing in me that says, I can do without God, I don't need Him. The hatred of the world has its source there." [1]

–Oswald Chambers (1874-1917)

CHAPTER 4
IN GOD WE TRUST?
God's Perfect Word and His Imperfect People

SIN STARTS SMALL

Gen. 3:1-2 *Now the serpent was the most cunning of all the wild animals that the Lord God had made. He said to the woman, "Did God really say, 'You can't eat from any tree in the garden'?" The woman said to the serpent, "We may eat the fruit from the trees in the garden."*

IMAGINE YOUR PARENTS WALK YOU into the kitchen one day and have a serious talk with you that goes something like this: "We want you to know that we love you. We want the best for you. That's why we have given you free reign of the kitchen. You can eat everything in the refrigerator that you want. The pantry, too. Any time you need a snack, just come on in. But there's one thing. Up there on the shelf, there is a jar of cookies. Those are bad for you. There are plenty of other cookies in the pantry that you can help yourself to, just please keep your hands off that one jar."

This would be a totally different scenario than if you were starving, and your parents brought you into the kitchen and laughed at your hunger. They opened up all the cabinets and showed you that even though you were hungry, there was no food in the house. Then they put a steaming hot plate of chocolate chip cookies in front of you and told you not to eat them.

In the first scenario, your parents have provided for you. They love you. Their command about the cookies, though you might not fully understand it, is built on that love. You know it's true.

But in the second scene, your parents are misers. They withhold things just to be mean. They enjoy their power over you and abuse it for their enjoyment.

The great lie of Satan in Genesis 3 made Adam and Eve think about God in terms of the second scenario rather than the first. He talked about God like He was a withholder rather than a provider. And the first humans succumbed to the temptation. They believed the lie about God, and their behavior was devastating.

Sin, at its core, is about disbelief. We sin because we don't really believe God loves us. That He wants the best for us. That He's not withholding from us. But if that's true, then the way you fight sin isn't just to try hard against it. It's to remind yourself of what is true about God. Today, when you are tempted, don't just try and say no. Remember who God is, and use that memory to stand strong.

PAUSE AND REFLECT

▷ **What does freedom in Christ mean?**

▷ **Would you describe Adam and Eve as being free or restricted? Why?**

▷ **What about you? Do you find freedom in Christ or restrictions? What has caused that feeling?**

ALMOST ISN'T ENOUGH

Gen. 3:2-5 *The woman said to the serpent, "We may eat the fruit from the trees in the garden. But about the fruit of the tree in the middle of the garden, God said, 'You must not eat it or touch it, or you will die.'" "No! You will not die," the serpent said to the woman. "In fact, God knows that when you eat it your eyes will be opened and you will be like God, knowing good and evil."*

WHAT IS THE ONE MOVIE that you have seen more than any other? Are you thinking of it? Right now, you could probably pick up the dialogue from any point in that movie. In fact, you may have incorporated phrases from the film into your regular conversation. That's your movie; you know it backward and forward.

In fact, you have such a personal attachment to that movie that you get offended when people try and quote it, only to butcher what you know to be the true words. But that's how personally you know it. That's how closely you are attached to it.

As you read the encounter between the serpent and Eve in Genesis 3, notice that the serpent questioned the word of God. And Eve seemed at first to defend those words. But if you read carefully, you'll see that when Eve quoted God back to the serpent, she "almost" got it right.

Almost, but not quite.

And in this case, almost isn't good enough. The troubling thing for most of us is that Satan might actually have a better grasp on the Word of God than we do. He knows who God is, and He knows what God said. If we want to be serious about defending attacks from the devil, we had better know what God said, too.

Not almost know. Not sort of know.

Know. Exactly.

And why shouldn't we? We memorize everything else: song lyrics, movie lines, favorite quotes—why not the Bible? Could it be that we simply don't have the same personal attachment to Scripture that we do to so many other things?

PAUSE AND REFLECT

▷ How well you do know God's Words?

▷ What keeps you from enjoying time with God and His Word?

▷ Could it be that Satan knows the Word of God better than you do?

▷ What changes do you need to make to reverse that?

DON'T TREAT THE SYMPTOMS

Gen. 3:6 *Then the woman saw that the tree was good for food and delightful to look at, and that it was desirable for obtaining wisdom. So she took some of its fruit and ate it; she also gave some to her husband, who was with her, and he ate it.*

THE CORE ISSUE IN GENESIS 3 is the same core issue at stake in any temptation. It's not sex. It's not food. It's not anger. It's not greed.

It's trust.

When you go to the doctor, there is always a moment when you list your symptoms. Those symptoms are carefully recorded, and when taken together, they lead to a diagnosis. Often, the symptoms aren't really the problem. They are the surface-level manifestations of something deeper going on inside of you. That's why the solution to a runny nose isn't a Kleenex, it's an antibiotic. A good doctor doesn't settle with treating the symptoms. He looks deeper.

Such is the case with us. We must look deeper, past the surface-level temptations and into the area of trust. When we are tempted toward materialism, the real issue is whether we trust that God has and will provide enough. Are we content with what He provides? When we are tempted toward sex, the real issue is whether we trust God when He gives us the prescribed means of sex in marriage. Do we believe what God is telling us or what culture is selling? When we are tempted to overeat, the deeper issue is whether we trust God when He says that our bodies are temples of the Holy Spirit. Are we willing to treat our bodies as such?

And fighting these temptations? Well, that's an issue of trust, too. Do we really trust that God will give us the grace to stand firm, or are we relying on our own strength? It all comes down to trust. So who are you trusting today? Take a look at your actions. They're the symptoms and they will lead you to the truth.

PAUSE AND REFLECT

▷ When it comes to resisting sin, who are you trusting?

▷ Think about the nagging sin present in your life right now. What is the real issue behind that sin? What are you trading or looking for when you give in to that sin?

▷ How can Christ satisfy that need better?

IN GOD WE TRUST?

Rather than trusting God's Word, we question it, belittle it, and disobey it.

"IN GOD WE TRUST." We see these words on American currency. We hear these words in patriotic songs such as "The Star-Spangled Banner." The phrase was adopted as the national motto of the United States of America in 1956. Trust is a serious matter. America's national motto implies both that we are dependent and that God is trustworthy. But do we really trust God?

In the fall of 2008, the unthinkable happened: the "almighty dollar" (as many have dubbed it) was weakened through a series of economic trends that brought the U.S. economy to the brink of disaster. Ironically, as the value of the dollar shrunk, it became apparent that many people had been trusting in *it* rather than God. The motto turned out to be mere words with very little truth behind them.

The issue of trust goes to the heart of what it means to be human. As we have seen in previous lessons, God has revealed Himself through what He has created as well as through His Word. God is not silent. He has spoken to us and recorded His words in the Bible. But are we listening? And when we encounter His word, do we really trust Him?

The Bible teaches that God spoke into being all that exists. The pinnacle of creation is mankind—made in His own image (Gen. 1:27). Then God proclaimed all that He created to be "very good" (v. 31), thus affirming that all of creation was fulfilling His intended purposes.

Because God created by His words and because all that He created was "very good," we know that *God's words are the source of all that is good. Therefore, God's words can and must be trusted*. Initially, God's image-bearers, Adam and Eve, enjoyed a relationship with God as obedient worshipers trusting His good words. "In God We Trust" would have been an appropriate motto for those early days in the Garden of Eden.

As you read through the following questions, think about who or what your first, initial answer is. As you think about your answer, ask yourself why you answered that way and what does it say about who I trust.

- If your car broke down on your way home from a friend's house, whom would you call?
- You just found out your parents are getting a divorce. Whom do you call?

- You mother is a stay at home mom, and your dad just lost his job. What is your first reaction?
- You're about to board an airplane but realize you have no idea if the pilot has checked everything out or if the plane is safe. Do you get on the plane?
- Your teacher provides a study guide for an upcoming test. She says everything on the test will be covered by the study guide. Do you spend any time going back through your notes or reading more in your book?
- Your doctor prescribes a medicine you have never heard of. Do you research it first or just take how many he said to take?
- The Bible tells you that God has a plan for your life. You know that plan doesn't include many things that will happen at a certain party you have been invited to. Do you go?
- Each of these questions deals with trust. We place trust in others all the time without even realizing it. Why do we find it so easy to trust others and so difficult to trust God?

In this lesson, we see how our fallen nature came from and results in mishandling God's special revelation—His Word. Our goal is to believe the trustworthiness of God and His Word so that we might grow in worship and obedience through learning to handle God's Word faithfully.

So let's look at Genesis 3:1-6 and see how Adam and Eve's misdirected worship is rooted in the way they handled God's spoken word. By looking at the actions of Adam and Eve, we can see our own tendency to rebel against God's written Word by putting our trust in ourselves rather than in God. Can we really say that we trust, worship, and obey God when we question, belittle, and disobey God's Word?

RATHER THAN TRUSTING GOD'S WORD...

▶ WE QUESTION IT (GEN. 3:1-2).

¹Now the serpent was the most cunning of all the wild animals that the LORD God had made. He said to the woman, "Did God really say, 'You can't eat from any tree in the garden'?"

²The woman said to the serpent, "We may eat the fruit from the trees in the garden."

Early in the biblical narrative, we find Adam and Eve facing temptation from a crafty and deceitful serpent in the Garden of Eden. Many people have missed the point of this historical encounter by focusing on where the serpent came from, what type of fruit he was offering, and whose fault the whole debacle really was. While those questions may be interesting, they are not ones that God deemed crucial to us fulfilling our purpose of living as worshipers in obedience to His Word.

Whenever we approach Scripture, our primary question should be "What does this text say about God?" This particular passage makes clear that the serpent was among the creatures that God made. We know from Genesis 1–2 that God made everything "good," meaning that everything originally functioned according to His purposes.

But this serpent entered the garden in order to disrupt the peace of God's creation. At this point, the Bible does not tell us where the serpent came from or who he is. What we do know is that the serpent is crafty. Theologian D. A. Carson notes that the word "crafty" entails "sneakiness…[or] someone who is wise and prudent." Part of the "goodness" God bestowed on the being later identified as Satan (literally, "the accuser") is wisdom or prudence. Carson expands: "The serpent, Satan, was crowned with more prudence than all the other creatures, but in his rebelling the prudence became craftiness; the very same virtue that was such a strength became twisted into a vice."[4]

The serpent displayed his twisted wisdom by subtly attacking God's word and maligning God's character. The serpent spoke: "Did God really say?" The irony of this scene is heavy. The Bible began with God speaking all things into existence—including the serpent. And now the serpent that was created by the word of God has questioned the authority of the One whose word created him! With this subtle question, he usurped the clearly communicated word of God.

"Did *God* really say?" the serpent asked. Some people do not obey God's Word because they do not believe it to be *God's* Word. They reject the Word because they see no authority behind it.

Imagine this scene. A group of schoolchildren are enjoying recess time on the playground. The teacher sits quietly on the bench near the swing set. When it's time to go back to class, she tells one of the students to call the others inside. If the children are having a wonderful time, some of them will question the source of their classmate's message. "Who said we have to go in now?" they ask. "The teacher said so!" comes the reply. "Did the teacher really say we have to leave now? How do we know?" they persist. Their desire to stay on the playground will cause them to question the authority of the messenger.

In a similar manner, the serpent planted a seed of doubt in Eve's mind regarding the source of authority: "Did *God* really say that?" He knew that if she doubted the source of the command, she would disregard it.

"Did God really say?" the serpent asked. Eve responded rightly: "YES! He did." In Genesis 2:16-17, God explicitly commanded Adam not to eat of the tree of the knowledge of good and evil. The serpent's question undermined the holy authority of God and maligned the loving character of God.

God's word had not restricted Adam and Eve uncaringly; rather, His command offered amazingly abundant choices. In the garden, the man and woman had endless opportunities for obeying God by eating the fruit from any of the other trees. There was only one solitary possibility for disobedience. But it was at the point of the restriction that the serpent made his crafty attack. Eve's response was at least initially hopeful, for she recognized the serpent's subtle error and corrected him. She also maintained the source of the command as being from God. However, in her correction we learn something about ourselves.

▶ **WE BELITTLE IT (GEN. 3:2-5).**

² The woman said to the serpent, "We may eat the fruit from the trees in the garden. ³ But about the fruit of the tree in the middle of the garden, God said, 'You must not eat it or touch it, or you will die.' "

⁴ "No! You will not die," the serpent said to the woman. ⁵ "In fact, God knows that when you eat it your eyes will be opened and you will be like God, knowing good and evil."

As this conversation unfolded, Eve's own doubts emerged in the form of her adding a harsh exaggeration to God's word: "But about the fruit of the tree in the middle of the garden, God said, 'You must not eat it *or touch it*, or you will die' " (v. 3). Eve belittled God's word by adding to it. Her addition to the word of God misrepresented God as a harsh taskmaster.

Some skeptics belittle God's Word by *subtracting* from it. The third president of the United States of America, Thomas Jefferson, created his own "Bible." He described the process of creating "his" version: "We must reduce our volume to the simple evangelists, select, even from them, the very words only of Jesus…I have performed this operation for my own use, by cutting verse by verse out of the printed book, and arranging the matter…as diamonds in a dunghill."⁵

Others reduce God's Word by *adding* to it. Joseph Smith, the founder of Mormonism, added to God's Word by claiming that an angel had given him *The Book of Mormon*. The Bible alone wasn't enough, so Joseph Smith felt the need to expand on what God had already delivered.

These are extreme examples, but the error of both is the same as that of Eve. Her posture toward the word of God demonstrated her desire for independence.

D.A. Carson writes: "A lot of people think that 'sin' is: just breaking a rule. What is at stake here is something deeper, bigger, sadder, uglier, more heinous. It is a revolution. It makes me god and thus de-gods God."[6] Far too often we don't view sin in this way.

When Satan can't get us to undermine God's Word through outright unbelief, he will try to get us to undermine it through misplaced trust. That's why Eve began to speak authoritative words herself—words that painted God in a negative light. From this account we learn that one of the great dangers we face when handling the Word of God is the temptation to place ourselves in the seat of authority over it.

The encounter between the serpent and Eve continued as the serpent then openly defied God's word: "No! You will not die," the serpent said to the woman. "In fact, God knows that when you eat it your eyes will be opened and you will be like God, knowing good and evil" (vv. 4-5).

Satan has now shown his cards. What started as subtle skepticism has become outright rebellion. Satan has implied that God is a liar. Furthermore, he has undermined the character of God by leading Adam and Eve to believe that God was withholding goodness from them. Graeme Goldsworthy explains it this way: "Eating the forbidden fruit did indeed mean that the humans came to know good and evil (Gen. 3:22). But the process by which they achieved that involved a rebellion against truth and its source. Instead of knowing good and evil by rejecting evil and remaining good, they chose rather to reject good and become evil…[Satan] does not suggest that the humans transfer their allegiance from God to himself, but only that they themselves should consider and evaluate God's claim to truth." [8]

Our postmodern infatuation with entertainment and social media highlights our desire to make our own truth claims. Facebook has the "Like" button. Twitter has a "Retweet" button. Both are geared toward receiving the praise of men through their affirmation of one's fleeting expression—whether truthful or not. Today there is even a site that uses public opinion through voting to settle personal disputes about truth claims. The site boasts, "Have a disagreement with someone? Settle it here!" "Everything's Debatable." "Just upload your 30 second argument and let the viewers decide who's right." Just imagine for a moment how crazy things might be if God's Word came to us with this kind of website as its medium! But then again, whenever we allow either personal preference or public opinion to shape our understanding of truth, we are standing in judgment over God in much the same way.

▶ WE DISOBEY IT (GEN. 3:6).

⁶Then the woman saw that the tree was good for food and delightful to look at, and that it was desirable for obtaining wisdom. So she took some of its fruit and ate it; she also gave some to her husband, who was with her, and he ate it.

God had spoken very plainly to Adam in Genesis 2:17 regarding this prohibited tree. Often men will begin to play the "blame game"—"It was Eve's fault!" We see this unfold in Genesis 3:12. Adam blamed Eve, and in some sense he also blamed God: "The woman *You* gave to be with me…" In 1 Timothy 2:14, it seems that Paul affirmed that it was Eve who was deceived. But Paul also said in 1 Corinthians 11:3 that man is the head, or steward, over the woman. God had given the commandment to Adam—*before* Eve was taken from his side. It was Adam's responsibility to teach and protect Eve. But we find Adam standing nearby—silent and complicit.

The point of this story is not about the type of fruit, as if the fruit juices would poison the minds of Adam and Eve. No, the poison of sin coursed through their veins before the fruit entered their mouths. "It was not the nature of the tree that made it dangerous, the bearer of covenant curse and death, but what it stood for: obedience to the word of God."[10]

We know that the serpent, Adam, and Eve all transgressed God's command. Each of them was guilty of disobeying God's word, as are we. And every time we choose to disobey, we are proclaiming to God that we are wiser than He is. We are "crafty" and we deserve condemnation.

What happened in the garden is replayed in our own lives every single day. Often when we are tempted, we wonder, *Did God really say?* Our answer to that question is illustrative of whom we really trust and whom we really worship. When Adam and Eve questioned, belittled, and disobeyed God's word, they went from being awestruck worshipers of God to being brazen idolaters worshiping themselves.

Worship is at stake in how we approach the Word of God. How we handle and respond to God's Word will show whom we worship.

▶ CONCLUSION

There is only one person who lived a life that demonstrated without reservation the truth of this statement: "In God I trust." He too was put to the test like Adam and Eve.

God placed Adam into a lush garden with endless possibilities to worship and obey and only one prohibition. God drove Jesus into the wilderness where He had no food, water, or shelter. And there Jesus came face to face with that crafty serpent who used the same game plan—to get Jesus to question, belittle, and disobey God's Word.

How did Jesus respond? By affirming His trust in God's Word. By uplifting the true intent of God's Word. By obeying God's Word. There in the wilderness, Jesus succeeded where Adam and Eve had failed. Jesus perfectly fulfilled God's purpose *for us*—He worshiped and obeyed the Father by trusting His Word. And when Jesus laid down His life as an atoning sacrifice for us on the cross, His perfect worship and obedience were made available to us.

QUESTIONS

1. What do the words "In God We Trust" mean to you? Do those words accurately reflect the way you live? Why or why not?

2. What are some examples of how man has taken things that God made "good" and used them for evil purposes? What are some virtues that Satan twists into vices?

3. What are some reasons people deny the truth that God inspired the Scriptures? Is it possible that some of us deny the authorship of Scripture because we do not want Scripture to have authority in our lives?

4. How has our culture's obsession with "being true to ourselves" or "being independent" affected our view of God and His Word?

5. When you think of sin, what do you generally consider it? Disobedience or Revolution? How do they differ?

6. How might both public opinion and personal preference negatively shape your understanding of God and His Word?

7. In what way is questioning God's Word different from asking questions of God's Word?

8. Why does our sin imply that we are wiser than God? When we sin, why do we think we can fill a void with something other than God? How temporarily is that void filled?

9. What are some examples of times in your life when you were forced to answer the question "Did God really say?" How did you respond to the temptation to distrust God?

10. Whom are you trusting in today? Self? Public opinion? Jesus? How is that playing out in your life?

CHAPTER 5
GOD'S LAW FOR LIFE
God Reveals His Standard of Obedience

HIS PEOPLE, HIS STANDARDS

Ex. 20:1-2 *Then God spoke all these words: I am the Lord your God, who brought you out of the land of Egypt, out of the place of slavery.*

HAVE YOU EVER STAYED UP late working on a paper because it was due the next day? You finish typing as the sun comes up and struggle with the printer, because they never work right when you are late for something. You rush everything else to make sure you are in class on time to turn in your masterpiece. You haven't slept for what feels like days, you need a shower, but you made it. You turned your paper in on time. As class starts, you proudly hand in your paper. Most of the class is prepared, but a couple of students aren't. Rather than docking their grade, the teacher simply says not to worry about the paper. How do you feel now? Has your attitude toward the teacher changed? Does it seem right that some students were allowed to not turn it in? You learn something about the character of the teacher by how he handles that situation.

When it comes to God, the behaviors, attitudes, and expectations He has for us, which are set forth in His Law, serve as a reflection of His own character. If God were to be unconcerned about our wicked ways, what would that indicate about His own character? It would not reflect the fact that He is holy, righteous, and just in all His ways. But when God is appalled at our idolatry, lying, stealing, murdering, and coveting, we begin to grasp something of His own nature and character.

Throughout Scripture we see and learn about the character attributes of God. He is described as the highest measure of all wisdom, love, righteousness, justice, jealousy, wrath, mercy, and other attributes. But the only attribute that is used three successive times to describe God's character is "holy." In Isaiah 6:3 the prophet gets a peek of the throne room of God and hears the angels declaring to one another, "Holy, holy, holy is the Lord of Hosts." When describing what their eyes beheld, the angels only described one attribute of God: holy. Because our Triune God is holy holy holy, He must set forth a moral standard which reflects that holiness. When we read the Law and see what God expects of us in our character, we learn about His own character. He is the One True God, holy in all His ways, and He calls us to be holy as He is holy (Lev. 20:26).

PAUSE AND REFLECT

▷ As His people, why do we think we should determine the standard?

▷ Since you have no capability to be holy, what do you do?

▷ How can you achieve His standard?

GOD'S LAW TEACHES US HOW TO RELATE TO GOD AND OTHERS

Do not have other gods besides Me.
Do not make an idol for yourself.
Do not misuse the name of the LORD your God.
Remember the Sabbath day, to keep it holy.
Honor your father and your mother.
Do not murder.
Do not commit adultery.
Do not steal.
Do not give false testimony against your neighbor.
Do not covet.

For an exact reading of the 10 Commandments, see Ex. 20:3-17

THERE ARE FEW THINGS WORSE than being ignorant of the expectations. Can you imagine starting a class and not knowing your teacher's expectations? Imagine coming in and being clueless about what your teacher wants you to accomplish. Envision the end of the year approaching and your teacher walks up one day to inform you that you have failed the class. Yes, you did well on the exams, but you failed to meet additional requirements and will be forced to repeat the class. I suspect you would be a little frustrated that you were never told what was expected of you.

In life, we will find ourselves in situations and circumstances where non-communicated expectations exist. It happens in relationships with friends, parents, teachers, and employers. In those situations, where we are being held accountable to non-communicated expectations, we have a right to voice our concerns. However, when it comes to God's standard of expectations, we are not clueless. God has not left us without instruction on how we are to relate to Him or others.

God's law teaches us about how we are to walk with Him through life. We do not have to wonder what He expects of us—we can turn to His Word, look at His Law, and see His expectations. Not only are we informed about how to walk with Him, but also how to treat others. We know what is forbidden and what is encouraged. May we be people who look to God's perfect Law to guide us in how we are to relate to God and others.

PAUSE AND REFLECT

▷ **Do you find freedom and love in God setting His expectations or do you find slavery?**

▷ **How can a list of restrictions be loving? Protective?**

▷ **Have your parents ever prohibited you from doing something or going somewhere and later you were thankful they did?**

GOD ASKS FOR COMPLETE OBEDIENCE

MANY ASSUME THAT BECAUSE GOD has forgiven the sins of those who have repented and placed faith in Jesus, that He must have somehow lowered the standard. This is not true. The standard of God is perfection. Jesus says in Matthew 5:48, "Be perfect, therefore, as your heavenly Father is perfect." Jesus is not speaking metaphorically when he tells us that the standard is perfection. He is showing the standard. He lived the standard and the exact same standard is expected of us.

Complete perfection is the expectation by which God judges, and will judge, every human being. That means you, just in case you were wondering. With that in mind, think back over your last 24 hours. How many times did you fall short of perfection? Please note it only takes one mistake to erase perfection. Just like in sports, one loss means you aren't undefeated. One loss isn't bad, but it isn't perfect. This whole ordeal brings to light our desperate situation. We are not perfect. Many believe that God judges based on the measuring scale of our good deeds versus our bad ones. If the good outweighs the bad, we are good. But James 2:10 reminds us that, "For whoever keeps the entire law, yet fails in one point, is guilty of breaking it all." This means that even one breaking of the law has burdened us with the responsibility and guilt of all of it.

This is why we need grace. Grace is unmerited favor. God shows us unmerited favor by choosing to treat us as Christ deserved to be treated: as a son. And he treated Christ as we deserve to be treated: as law-breaking sinners. God never lowers the standard of perfection for salvation; instead he imputes to us the perfection of His Son and imputes to His Son our unrighteousness. This is grace and yes, it is quite amazing!

PAUSE AND REFLECT

▷ As you think about the standard God requires and the punishment for falling short, do you appreciate what Jesus did for you a little more?

▷ He didn't suffer figuratively, He suffered physically for you. How does this change your affection toward Him?

▷ How can you demonstrate your affection for Christ?

GOD'S LAW FOR LIFE:

God's moral standard reflects his character, guides all relationships and reveals our need for grace.

IMAGINE THAT YOUR PARENTS are planning to adopt an infant from an impoverished country. You spend weeks preparing the house to welcome this new child into the family. You even give up your room and allow it to be turned into the nursery. You don't mind taking the smaller room because you want to show how much you love your future sister. The day finally arrives when you join your parents to visit the orphanage and bring home your new sister. When your family arrives at the orphanage, you find a malnourished baby girl living in a very run down facility. You are troubled to see the conditions she has been living in, but you are overjoyed to know that this will be her last day there. She's coming home!

Once you get back home, you can see your sister is having difficulty adjusting to her new surroundings. She's not used to bathing daily. She's unaccustomed to the food she is eating. She's a bit fussy because of all the changes. Nevertheless, you bear with her, showing great patience because, after all, she is *family* now. Seeing where she came from and where she is now, you are so happy your family decided to adopt.

Time passes and she grows into a little girl. Now, your parents begin teaching her the rules of the house. You used to think your parents were strict, but now you realize the rules they are setting in place are actually there to protect your little sister. They teach her what's best for her *and* for your family.

But one day, she begins to complain about the rules. "Dad and Mom, you're being mean to me! Why won't you let me do *this* or *that*?" She even gets angry at you when she feels you take their side. This is your baby sister—the same one that was rescued from a painful life that would've known little in the way of love. And now she is accusing your parents of being harsh for expecting obedience to such "strict rules"!

What your sister fails to realize, of course, is that if she not been adopted, she wouldn't be under these love-driven rules. She also wouldn't have a family that loves her. Instead, she would be under rules made by people who were not family. Or worse yet, she might have been put out on the streets by now with no protective relationships in place.

Stephen Lennox describes this scenario in his book, God's Story Revealed, noting that rules given to such a child convey the truth that they are no longer orphaned but are part of a family.[2]

THE BIBLICAL STORY LINE UNFOLDS

In the previous chapter, we learned how a crafty serpent with twisted wisdom tricked Adam and Eve into disobeying God's word. Man and Woman broke their relationship with the God who had made them in His image. Though their sin had cosmic consequences, God graciously revealed hope for fallen humanity by promising a Rescuer, the Seed of woman, who alone could fix what they had destroyed.

Mankind's sin and its effects quickly spread to every aspect of life. But in Genesis 12, God made a covenant promise to a man named Abraham: through his offspring, all the nations would be blessed. The remainder of Genesis traces his lineage and displays God's power to work through seemingly hopeless circumstances to keep His promises. Abraham's children (known collectively as Israel) settled in Egypt, not the land that was promised to their forefather.

When Exodus picks up the story, we find God's chosen people enslaved by Pharaoh in Egypt. God heard the cries of His people, and He chose a man named Moses to serve as a mediator while God Himself would rescue His people and keep His promise. God was coming to make an orphaned slave into His very own "treasured possession."

Once this rescue took place, God revealed that His people's new identity would involve living under a new standard of conduct. God was about to "lay down the law," revealing to His people crucial distinguishing aspects of His own identity as well as aspects of their new identity as His people.

God's moral standard...

▶ **REFLECTS HIS CHARACTER (EX. 20:1-2).**

¹Then God spoke all these words: ²I am the LORD your God, who brought you out of the land of Egypt, out of the place of slavery.

Have you ever gotten "the silent treatment" from someone? Or have you ever known someone who talks all of the time without saying much at all? The ability to communicate is part of what it means to be made in God's image. We have been given the ability to communicate with God and with one another. Lack of clear communication usually means trouble for a relationship.

In Exodus 20, we see God communicating clearly (through Moses) to all of Israel about His expectations of them. These are not merely the ideas of Moses, these are the words of God, and as such, they carry the authority and importance of their true Author.

D. A. Carson notes that "(God) is still being presented as a talking God, not only with the kind of speech that calls the universe into existence (Genesis 1–2) and with the kind of speech that interacts with his image-bearers (Genesis 3)…but with the kind of speech that commands them."[5]

Everyone lives by some moral standard. In our own postmodern era, many people describe truth as relative or unknowable. But even they are making a truth claim that shapes the way they make moral decisions. Though the Bible is more than just a book of rules, it does indeed make claims that should shape the lives of those who call themselves "Christian."

When it comes to God's people, God does not just leave the issue of right and wrong for us to decide. He has a righteous standard that flows out of who He is. If we are to be in relationship with God, we must come to Him on *His* terms and not our own.

Israel had to learn this lesson. The Israelites had long been living under the authority of Pharaoh and his idolatrous laws. Their life in Egypt affected the way they thought about their own identity. Egyptian culture influenced the way they lived. For example, the Egyptians upheld Pharaoh as a semi-divine being. His authority over the residents of his kingdom was grounded in his being like a god to them. Pharaoh had long portrayed for Israel an improper understanding of God and a moral standard that ran contrary to God's. As a result, Israel's identity had been heavily influenced by Pharaoh's values. Israel had to "unlearn" certain falsehoods in order to see the world rightly and to live according to God's commands.

When we speak about someone's character, we sometimes use the phrase, "He's a man of his word" to describe trustworthiness. Sometimes politicians are accused of making "hollow promises," a term that means their words can't be trusted. Words are important because they convey the character of the person speaking them.

God is the Master Communicator. His law reflects His perfect moral character. God never speaks hollow words. Just as you can know what kind of father I am to my children by the words I speak to them, God's words reflect who He is. The rules He gives us reflect His character as a loving Father.

Consider the first words Moses recorded when God spoke the Ten Commandments: "I am the LORD your God." This is covenant language that carries with it not only a statement of fact but of promise. God has revealed Himself to Moses and now to all Israel as "YHWH," or "I AM." He is the eternal and unchanging God.

Watch what comes next. See how God's name becomes synonymous with what He has done for Israel: "I am the LORD your God, who brought you out of the land of Egypt, out of the place of slavery." Though He is the God of all nations, He established a unique relationship with Israel. He became her Redeemer and Rescuer so that she would be His own possession, a kingdom of priests and holy people. This is the relationship that forms the foundation for all of the Ten Commandments. It is precisely because He has rescued her and restored relationship with her that He demands moral fidelity from her. Israel's new identity is now tied to God's identity!

God did not just deliver Israel from the bondage of Egypt, He delivered them into His own presence! They were saved *from* slavery *for* God. God's love is signified not only in His delivering us from the bondage of sin but also in His expectations of fidelity from us. Failure to have those expectations would convey apathy and lack of affection, that we don't really belong to Him.

God's law was a gift to Israel that told them how to live as God's chosen people. Ultimately, Israel's obedience would make them a "light to the nations" (Isa. 42:6; 49:6) and a "city on a hill" (Matt. 5:14) so that God's global plan of redemption would advance to all peoples. But even with this view of ultimate redemption in place, the law also teaches us how to relate to God and others.

▶ GUIDES ALL RELATIONSHIPS (EX. 20:3-17).

If we are going to understand God's purpose in giving the Ten Commandments, then we need to see how they are structured. The first four focus vertically on our relationship to God. The last six focus horizontally on our relationship to others. Together, they guide every relationship we could have.

Jesus may have alluded to this structure when He answered the question in Matthew 22:36-40 regarding which command is most important. Jesus quoted Deuteronomy 6:5, "Love the LORD your God with all your heart, with all your soul, and with all your strength." This summarizes the vertical nature of commandments 1-4.

Then Jesus went on to emphasize Leviticus 19:18: "Love your neighbor as yourself." This summarizes the horizontal nature of commandments 5-10. It seems Jesus was saying that the two orientations, God-ward and man-ward, are tied together. Let's read Exodus 20:3-11, noting the vertical dimension of the first four commandments.

³ Do not have other gods besides Me.

⁴ Do not make an idol for yourself, whether in the shape of anything in the heavens above or on the earth below or in the waters under the earth. ⁵ You must not bow down to them or worship them; for I, the LORD your God, am a jealous God, punishing the children for the fathers' sin, to the third and fourth generations of those who hate Me, ⁶ but showing faithful love to a thousand generations of those who love Me and keep My commands.

⁷ Do not misuse the name of the LORD your God, because the LORD will not leave anyone unpunished who misuses His name.

⁸ Remember the Sabbath day, to keep it holy: ⁹ You are to labor six days and do all your work, ¹⁰ but the seventh day is a Sabbath to the LORD your God. You must not do any work—you, your son or daughter, your male or female slave, your livestock, or the foreigner who is within your gates. ¹¹ For the LORD made the heavens and the earth, the sea, and everything in them in six days; then He rested on the seventh day. Therefore the LORD blessed the Sabbath day and declared it holy.

Now let's read Exodus 20:12-17, noting the horizontal relational dimension of commandments 5-10.

¹² Honor your father and your mother so that you may have a long life in the land that the LORD your God is giving you. ¹³Do not murder. ¹⁴ Do not commit adultery. ¹⁵ Do not steal. ¹⁶ Do not give false testimony against your neighbor. ¹⁷ Do not covet your neighbor's house. Do not covet your neighbor's wife, his male or female slave, his ox or donkey, or anything that belongs to your neighbor.

Just as the commandments have both a vertical and horizontal orientation, violation of the commandments has both consequences.

Take King David, for example. One evening, he went out on his rooftop and saw a beautiful woman bathing. He wanted her for himself (coveting). He took her and had sex with her (theft and adultery). He lied about it (false testimony). He had her husband killed to cover it up (murder).

But in his prayer of confession, he told God, "Against You—You alone—I have sinned and done this evil in Your sight" (Ps. 51:4). In keeping with the structure of the Ten Commandments, David's transgression of commandments 6-10 was rooted in his pride and violation of the spirit of the first four. Break one commandment and it's like a house of cards: they all come tumbling down!

When properly understood, God's law provides freedom within its constraints and boundaries. Turn these commandments around and you see the freedom that comes from keeping them. You are free to love and commune with the only God who is really God! You are free to love others above yourself!

Remember the household rules for the adopted child? These rules not only display a new identity for the child, they also grant a tremendous amount of freedom. Possibilities in life are opened up to the child that would have otherwise been unrealized simply because that child is now part of a new family.

We've seen that the law God gave His people revealed His character and His grace. It also revealed His people's inability to live up to His standard of righteousness. It is precisely because the law reveals God's *goodness* that it also reveals our *badness*. And as we see our sinfulness, we begin to feel our need for grace.

▶ REVEALS OUR NEED FOR GRACE.

The apostle Paul notes in Romans 3:23 that all of humanity has fallen short of God's standard set forth in the law. Even partial obedience equals complete disobedience. James 2:10 says, "For whoever keeps the entire law, yet fails in one point, is guilty of breaking it all."

As we saw in the previous lesson, obedience to God's Word displays trust in God's character. Conversely, disobedience is always rooted in distrust of God. We don't really believe that His way of living is best for us.

When we honestly examine our lives, it doesn't take long to recognize that we fail to measure up to God's standard as given in the law. All too often, however, we address this failure by trying harder to change our "actual practice," which results in legalism. If we are to avoid legalism, it is crucial that we view the law through the lens of the gospel.

God's purpose for the law was always to lead us to Christ. Paul states, "No one is justified by the works of the law but by faith in Jesus Christ" (Gal. 2:16). So what, then, was the point of the law? In Romans, Paul answers, "The law came along to multiply the trespass" (5:20). "The commandment that was meant for life resulted in death for me" (7:10).

▶ THE GOSPEL PROVIDES THE POWER FOR MISSION

Simply put, God gave these explicit standards and demanded obedience in order to show us our need for Christ. In speaking of the law, Jesus said, "Don't assume that I came to destroy the Law or the Prophets. I did not come to destroy but to fulfill" (Matt. 5:17).

Where Adam and Moses and every other human that has ever lived have failed, Christ succeeded. So then, "What the law could not do since it was limited by the flesh, God did. He condemned sin in the flesh by sending His own Son...in order that the law's requirement would be accomplished in us" (Rom. 8:3-4).

God's law is rooted in His own character. God is holy, and thus, His law is holy. And God demands holiness through *faith that produces obedience*, not the other way around. The gospel view of the law is that God provided in Christ all that He demands from us.

Our proper response is to believe it and then lean upon Him for our growth in obedience and to trust Him for the power to accomplish the mission He has given us.

Ed Stetzer and Philip Nation write: "The death of Christ upon the Cross makes it possible for missional believers to live lives of love. Perhaps we could even say, if we aren't on Christ's mission of love, we are looking down at the work of the Cross, not fully understanding it. We are ignoring its implications. The endgame for us ought to be a life within us that is different because of the presence of the Savior who died and rose for us."[15]

▶ CONCLUSION

Once upon a time, you were living as an orphan, destitute and impoverished with regard to God's righteous standard. But God came to you. He adopted you and gave you a new identity.

As He welcomed you into His family, He gave you guidelines to live by. The purpose of these laws is not to constrain you but rather to set you free to be everything He has created you to be. He requires total obedience, and He has granted all that He requires in Christ.

Some people view God's law as limiting rather than liberating, but within the Bible's story line, we can see the law as a description of a life of joyous freedom under the God who has made us. The law clearly explains God's standard for our relationship to Him and to others, spotlighting God's holiness while exposing our failures and faults. The law reveals our need for salvation but is powerless to save us. The gospel message is that even as God legislates, He points us to Jesus, who has kept the law in our place, thereby making our obedience possible.

QUESTIONS

1. How would you feel as the older sibling seeing your new sister rebel against the family that loves her? What rules are in place in your house that you don't like, but are there for your protection? Have you ever felt like the adopted girl in the story? What parallels are the between this story and gospel?

2. Why do many people have a deep aversion to the idea that God would command us to do or not do certain things? How can we demonstrate that God's moral standard is rooted in love?

3. If we are God's people, shouldn't we follow His directions for life? Does our identity shape our behavior or does our behavior shape our identity? How do identity and behavior relate to each other?

4. In what ways does understanding God's intention behind the law help us in our desire to be obedient? How does this keep us from reducing the law to just rules and regulations?

5. What are some examples we see in society of how breaking one commandment leads to breaking another? How has disobedience in one area of your life led to disobedience in other areas?

6. What freedoms are given through the Ten Commandments? In what ways do rules in your house actually provide freedom for you and your siblings? It is often easy to apply these thoughts to other people, but difficult to apply within our own family. What are some ways your disobedience here is impacting your relationships with your siblings?

7. In what ways do your stated beliefs and your actual practices contradict one another? Even though we believe certain actions to be wrong, we still do them. What does this tell us about our need for the gospel?

8. Consider the reasons for God's gift of the law. What does obeying God have to do with our mission as Christ's followers? How can we emphasize obedience in a way that makes clear the need for heartfelt, inside-out transformation and not merely legalism?

CHAPTER 6
NUMB TO THE WORD
Disobedience Leads to Death

DEATH SENTENCE

Rom. 6:23 *For the wages of sin is death, but the gift of God is eternal life in Christ Jesus our Lord.* **Eph. 2:1-2** *And you were dead in your trespasses and sins ²in which you previously walked according to the ways of this world, according to the ruler who exercises authority over the lower heavens, the spirit now working in the disobedient.*

EVERYONE LIKES FLOWERS. THEY'RE GREAT for impressing a date or for sitting on a bookshelf... at least for a while. But over the course of a few days, even the most beautiful flowers start to wither. The reason behind that withering is simple:

Flowers in a vase are dead.

Sure, they look good for a while. They have the appearance of life. But in the end, they are cut off at the stem, and without that link to the root, they are dead. Sure, they might show signs of life for a while, but that beauty is a lie. A wonderful lie, but a lie all the same.

This is an important spiritual truth for us to recognize. Too many people are flowers, not in a garden, but sitting in a vase. They may look pretty, even enhancing the beauty of the room they're sitting in, but that beauty is a lie. Though they have signs of life, they're actually spiritually dead; apart from Christ, all of us are cut off from the source of life. And it's just a matter of time until we start to show the signs of that death rather than life.

Verses like Ephesians 2:1-2 might sound at best pessimistic, and at worst mean, but these are words of love from the Lord. God loves us enough to tell us the truth about ourselves. He's not content to have us acting like we're alive; He wants us to be alive. The only way that life happens is through a living and vital connection to the vine of God in Christ.

PAUSE AND REFLECT

▷ Why is Ephesians 2:1-2 rooted in the love of God?

▷ What does it mean to be spiritually alive?

▷ Be honest with yourself, are you a flower in a garden or a vase?

PRIDE

Is. 64:6 *All of us have become like something unclean, and all our righteous acts are like a polluted garment; all of us wither like a leaf, and our iniquities carry us away like the wind.*

HAVE YOU EVER THOUGHT ABOUT what makes Christianity unique as a religion? You might think about stuff like the virgin birth, miracles, or the prophecies of the Old Testament, but think about this, too:

Christianity is the only religion that tells people how bad they are.

According to Emil Brunner, the Swiss theologian: "All other religions spare us the ultimate humiliation of being stripped naked and being declared bankrupt before God." That's pretty strong language.

And yet it points to the humiliating nature of Christianity. Other world religions don't treat humanity with such pessimism. In all other schools of thought, we have something to bring to the table. We can strive toward God and meet Him, and in a sense, be congratulated when we do.

Not Christianity.

In Christianity, we bring nothing to the table. In fact, the only thing we bring to the table with God is the sin we need to be rescued from. Perhaps that's why, if we look back into history, Christianity has been called the religion of women and slaves. In cultures of the past, neither of those two groups had many rights, so it wasn't a far stretch for them to admit their abject need of God's complete and total intervention on their behalf.

The bottom line is this: The one character flaw that has, and will continue to, keep most people from Christ is not greed. It's not lust. It's not lying or stealing or killing. It's pride. That's the only thing there is no room for at the foot of the cross.

PAUSE AND REFLECT

▷ **Why does pride, above all things, keep people from Jesus?**
▷ **Are you taking pride in your spiritual achievements today?**

TRANSPLANT

Rom. 3:10-12 *as it is written: There is no one righteous, not even one. There is no one who understands; there is no one who seeks God. All have turned away; all alike have become useless. There is no one who does what is good, not even one.*

Change is a natural part of life. You change classes. You change favorite songs. You change your underwear (hopefully). But the real discouraging news from the Bible is that there is one key thing that you cannot change:

You can't change your heart.

Think about it in terms of love. How would you tell someone how to love? Tricky question, right? You can tell someone how to behave, how to study, or how to set up a DVR, but how to love? That's much harder, and maybe even impossible. Love is a deep, heartfelt emotion that is backed up by choice and action. But because it's a condition, you can't make yourself do it. This is where the gospel starts to connect with us.

Jesus told us that the greatest commandment is to love God. And the second commandment is like it: to love other people. Here's the thing, though – because we can't change our hearts, we can't actually keep these two commandments Jesus gave us.

Jesus knows this, and that's why He doesn't tell us to change. He does the changing for us.

When you believe the gospel, you get a new heart, complete with new desires and affections. Now, you actually can love God, not because you made yourself do so, but because Jesus gave you the kind of heart that can.

PAUSE AND REFLECT

▷ Is it encouraging or discouraging to you that you can't change your heart?

▷ How does knowing that you can't change the heart change the way you talk about the gospel to others?

NUMB TO THE WORD

Our disobedience created a separation our actions can't repair and our desires can't overcome.

"UNCLEAN! UNCLEAN!" The shout resounded through the narrow streets of Palestine. Jewish ceremonial law rendered anyone with leprosy to be unclean. Any physical contact with lepers (even their shadow) would make you ceremonially unclean and exclude you from worship activities.

Why were lepers treated with such disdain? One reason concerned the disfigurement caused by the skin disease. A face without a nose is a scary sight. Fingers, toes, and other extremities were often missing. That's why anyone who had this infectious disease was considered an "outcast" by the rest of society. "Colonies" of lepers formed in order to provide social interaction for this ragged bunch of outcasts.

Leprosy is a disease that adversely affects the nervous system. It gradually numbs a person's extremities to the point at which pain is no longer felt. You might think that never feeling pain would be a good thing, right? After all, if you're going to get a filling in a tooth, you're thankful for that shot of Novocaine! And if you're going to have surgery, you schedule an anesthesiologist. Pain is bad, right? In the case of a cavity or a cut, we want to avoid needless pain. But what if the numbing from the Novocaine was permanent? What if the sensation of pain never returned to your mouth? Over time, you'd chew your tongue off!

Pain serves a purpose. In fact, it is a gift from God and part of His creation order. Pain tells a child not to touch a hot stove. Pain tells a carpenter to aim skillfully with a hammer. Pain warns and guides. And that's the problem with leprosy. Lepers are numb to pain, which means they don't know when their hand is burning or when they've just hit their thumb with a hammer. Lepers literally destroy their own bodies through their actions. Why? Because they can't feel anything. They don't sense that anything is wrong until it's too late.

But there's more to "feeling" than just pain. What about feeling good things? A leper doesn't feel pain. But neither can lepers feel the gentle touch of someone who cares for them. Numbness eliminates *all* feelings—the painful feelings given to protect you and the good feelings given to bless and encourage you. The numbness of leprosy results in "death by a thousand cuts." What a horrible disease!

More horrible than physical leprosy is spiritual numbness—the inability to recognize our sin and how it harms us and the inability to recognize God's grace and how it benefits us. Sin sears our consciences, leading us away from life—in all its beauty and complexity. The end result is spiritual death.

Last chapter, we discussed God's standard of conduct as given in the law. We saw that the Ten Commandments were given *after* God had already redeemed and rescued Israel from Egypt, putting an end to the idea that their obedience was what would save them. In Exodus 20, God spoke to the Israelites in order to show them how they should relate to Him vertically and how they should relate to one another horizontally.

Unfortunately, the remainder of the Old Testament painstakingly documents Israel's indifference to God's gracious Word. Where once it was Pharaoh who hardened his heart upon hearing the word of the Lord delivered through Moses, now the very people whom God had rescued chose to suppress the truth of God's Word. Israel's history is marked by cycles of disobedience, judgment, and deliverance.

The irony is that Israel's hearts proved to be much harder than the stone tablets upon which God had written His commands. But God promised through Jeremiah, "I will put My teaching within them and write it on their hearts. I will be their God, and they will be My people" (31:33). Spiritual leprosy would not have the last word!

Our disobedience...

▶ **CREATED A SEPARATION (EPH. 2:1-2; ROM. 6:23).**
¹ And you were dead in your trespasses and sins ² in which you previously walked according to the ways of this world, according to the ruler who exercises authority over the lower heavens, the spirit now working in the disobedient.
²³ For the wages of sin is death, but the gift of God is eternal life in Christ Jesus our Lord.

In Ephesians 2:1-2, we learn that we are spiritually dead. What does it look like for us to be dead in our trespasses and sins and to walk according to the ways of this world? The apostle Paul shines further light on this "spiritual deadness" in Romans 1–2. There he shows that we suppress the truth made available to us in general revelation (through creation) and also the truth made available to us in special revelation (God's direct Word to us).

So first, **we suppress the truth of general revelation**. This suppression comes out in several ways. For example, the pantheist declares that all of nature is God. The deist declares that God has nothing to do with the day-to-day workings of nature. Some people are so consumed with the creation that they fail to honor the Creator. Each of these positions is wrong, and they lead us to a warped view of creation and the Creator.

In His goodness, God has shown Himself to us in creation. But rather than glorify God or show gratitude, mankind has suppressed and disobeyed this God-speech and turned to idolatry. Our acts of suppression, disobedience, and idolatry always lead to death because they cut us off from the One through whom all life exists.

Second, **we suppress the truth of special revelation**, meaning we disregard God's direct Word to us. Paul often spoke of his own people as resting in their identity as God's chosen, in their possession of the law, in God's ownership of them, and in the ability to know His will. The tragedy was that God's people had abused these gifts and disobeyed God's law. If the Gentiles were guilty for suppressing their general knowledge of God, how much more the Jews for their outright disobedience of their special knowledge of God! What's worse, Jewish hypocrisy had resulted in God Himself being blasphemed.

Disobedience results in death. We exchange life for death. We rebel against God as our Master only to find we are now enslaved by another master—the Evil One. And our spiritual deadness leads to more and more sin. Our suppression of God's revelation shows that we don't value God's Word as we should. Because we don't recognize the value of God and His Word, we exchange the truth of God for a lie.

Like a naïve person in Chinatown paying top dollar for a "genuine" Rolex, our suppression of God's Word has made us speculators in the marketplace of sin. We have become comfortable trading in counterfeit currency—so comfortable that we are unable to recognize the voice of God apart from His gracious intervention.

If God's standard is perfect righteousness (and it is), and we are filled with all unrighteousness (and we are), then God's Word says that we deserve death. As we read above in Romans 6:23, Paul speaks of the wages earned by the sinner as being "death"—not just physical death, though that is certainly on the horizon. The death that Paul speaks of is the same death that God warned Adam about in Genesis 2:17— "you will certainly die." This is worse than physical death, which separates us from God's world. Paul is speaking here also of spiritual death, which separates us eternally from God Himself. Sin earns death.

▶ OUR ACTIONS CAN'T REPAIR (ISA. 64:6).

⁶ All of us have become like something unclean,
and all our righteous acts are like a polluted garment;
all of us wither like a leaf,
and our iniquities carry us away like the wind.

In the spring of 2011, Oprah Winfrey ended daily television show by hosting a variety of guests and celebrating the show's success. In the final few minutes, she took the stage much like a preacher. And the sermon to her adoring fans was about the root of our pain and suffering. She said: "There is a common thread that runs through all of our pain and all of our suffering, and that is unworthiness. Not feeling worthy enough to own the life you were created for. Even people who believe they deserve to be happy and have nice things often don't feel worthy once they have them." She went on to tell the audience: "Your being alive makes worthiness your birthright. You alone are enough."

Oprah's counsel to her massive television audience stands in direct contradiction to the Bible's view of our problem. Scripture doesn't teach us merely that we *feel* unworthy but that we *are* unworthy. And when we trace the signs of our brokenness and pain, we find the root cause of sin, and at the bottom of sin is unbelief.

All sin is rooted in unbelief. Each time we knowingly (or unknowingly) transgress God's righteous standard, we are doing so because we believe something (or someone) more than we believe God. The Greek word for "sin" carries the connotation of "missing the mark" as an archer might miss the bulls-eye on a target. The biblical authors go even further: We're not just missing the target, we are aimed in the opposite direction!

We're not just making mistakes. We are all filled with all unrighteousness, so that even the good things we do are tainted by unrighteous motives. No amount of cheerleading our own "worthiness" will make us truly worthy of God's love.

In Genesis 3, we read that after Adam and Eve sinned, they immediately made coverings for themselves in the form of fig leaves. This was a vain attempt to fix themselves. Why did they feel the need to cover their nakedness when just moments before, in Genesis 2:25, they "were naked, yet felt no shame"? The implicit reasoning is that once they suppressed the truth of God ("you will certainly die") and believed the lie of the serpent ("you will not die"), their eyes were opened and they now felt guilt and shame.

The feeling of guilt is a gift from God, much like nerve endings are to the human body. Guilt helps us avoid those things that are destructive in our lives. It is an internal working of the Spirit prompting the conscience when we abandon the righteous standard of God.

Shame is the emotional or physical response to guilt. When improperly handled, guilt and shame drive us deeper into sin by causing us to hide in the bushes, much like Adam and Eve. When the first man and woman covered themselves with fig leaves, it was because they recognized that they no longer met God's righteous standard. Fig leaves wither, thus making their efforts in vain. Had God not graciously replaced the leaves with skins, Adam and Eve would have been forced to cover themselves over and over in one act of vanity after another.

Isaiah 64 makes it clear that **no one will be saved because of personal effort**. Paul says the same in Romans 3:20: "For no one will be justified in His sight by the works of the law, because the knowledge of sin comes through the law."

Last chapter, when we discussed the role of the law and our response, it was clear that God didn't give us the law as a means to get right with Him through our effort. He gave the law to make us realize that we are broken and can't fix ourselves. Every time we transgress the law, if the Spirit of God is working in us, we feel that merciful twinge of guilt. Like a hot stove screams at your fingertips, "Move or my heat will destroy you!" the law of God shouts at transgressors like you and me: "You're not able! Run to Jesus!"

Rather than just sweep our sin under the rug and ignore it, God has dealt with it by sending His Son to bear its burden. Jesus is the righteousness of God, and those who put their trust in Him have the burden of their sin completely removed and receive the blessing of His righteous standing before the Father as their own! In 2 Corinthians 5:21, Paul said it this way: "He made the One who did not know sin to be sin for us, so that we might become the righteousness of God in Him." So our right standing with God is completely His own doing. The gospel removes any possibility for boasting (Rom. 3:27-28). Our only boast before God will be in the gift that He has given us—"eternal life in Christ Jesus our Lord" (6:23).

▶ OUR DESIRES CAN'T OVERCOME (ROM. 3:10-12).

10 as it is written: There is no one righteous, not even one.
11 There is no one who understands; there is no one who seeks God.
12 All have turned away; all alike have become useless. There is no one who does what is good, not even one.

When I was 14, I had a moment. I started to see that the way I was living did not line up with the stories that I heard in Sunday School. So I did what many people who are brought up in the Bible Belt do. I waited until the end of the worship service on a particular Sunday morning and went to the front. When our elderly pastor stepped down to greet me, I told him, "I want to straighten my life up." Unfortunately, my pastor replied by saying, "Okay. You're going to get baptized."

I left church that morning on cloud nine. I was ready to change! By evening, I had fallen from cloud nine without a parachute! But I went ahead and got baptized anyway, hoping that it would do some good. No change. Despite my best desires, I wasn't able to "straighten my life up." My best desires wouldn't save me.

In Romans 3, Paul quotes a number of Old Testament texts to drive home the point that "there is no one righteous…there is no one who seeks God" (Pss. 14:1-3;

53:1-3; Eccl. 7:20; Pss. 5:9; 140:3; 10:7; Isa. 59:7-8; Ps. 36:1). None of us really pursues God on our own.

But what about that neighbor who has been asking questions about church? What about those years that I listened to sermons and felt guilty? Are these not examples of seeking God? Yes and no. Yes, many people show interest in God long before their conversion. But no, that interest is not their doing. The bottom line is this: If a person is seeking God, it is because the Spirit is at work.

In Genesis 1–2, God created man and woman in His own image, and the result was nothing short of glorious. "Glory" carries the connotation of "weightiness." There was a glory to the man and woman in relation to the rest of creation because they reflected God's own glory. They had the distinct privilege of being God's steward over all that He had as they lived in perfect harmony with God. But then the man and woman fell from that glory. Their ability to accurately reflect God's glory was lost. They were still in His image, but that image was fractured. All creation suffered as a result. Mankind had "fallen short of the glory of God."

In the Old Testament, the people of Israel waited each year for the Day of Atonement for the assurance that their sins were forgiven. On that day, the high priest would take a blood sacrifice into the tent of meeting where God's presence dwelled, and he would sprinkle the blood on an altar called the holy of holies, where the glory of God rested. They had one chance. Everything was riding on one man to get the job done. But entering into the presence of God was terrifying because God's standard was perfect righteousness and nobody had it.

So take my personal scenario back into that mind-set. For me to "straighten my life up," I would have had to march right in there myself—and I would've fallen short of God's glory! According to the Scriptures, I would have dropped dead on the spot. Why? Even my best intentions to change are tainted with sin. On my best days, I still fail to live up to God's righteous standard. How could I enter into God's presence on my own when I was aimed in the wrong direction? I was indeed lost.

Thankfully, by the grace of God, my heart was not too hardened to hear from God. The Holy Spirit drew me into an authentic relationship with Christ when I was 21. I had grown numb, but Jesus stretched out his hand and touched me. Immediately, I was cleansed (Matt. 8:3).

▶ CONCLUSION

Humans were created to relate to God and one another. God has spoken clearly telling us how to live, but all too often, we ignore Him. We plug our ears and continue in the path of Frank Sinatra as if "doing it my way" works. All the while, God's Spirit convicts and prompts, beckoning us to repentance so that we may live. After a while, our hearts are so hard and calloused that they no longer feel conviction. We've become spiritual lepers! Like those in Jesus' day, lepers have a tendency of gathering together in shared misery.

The gospel says that Jesus still touches lepers—and when He does, feeling is restored. What was once disfigured and dead is made whole and alive! When we repent and turn to Christ at the sound of His voice, numbness flees and we are enabled to feel the pleasure of His love evermore in His presence.

You need no longer bear the internal pain of being "unclean." You have been made clean and now are free to gather with others who have been made clean in a new colony called the "church"—the people tasked with spreading the message of hope to a world of spiritual lepers.

Charles Spurgeon famously said that evangelism is nothing more than one beggar telling another beggar where to find bread. Applying Spurgeon's insight to leprosy, we might say God's mission goes forth when His people, whom He has healed of spiritual leprosy, go out and tell other spiritual lepers about the Savior who is willing to stretch out His hand and heal them too.

The church is a colony of former lepers. It's not a club for people who are perfect but an assembly of people who through God's grace have been forgiven and cleansed and whose lives are looking more and more like the Savior who healed them. We are no longer spiritual lepers whose lives are marked by uncleanness. Instead, the good news of Christ's healing power must resound from our lips and be demonstrated in our lives.

QUESTIONS

1. Have you ever felt numb to God's Word? What attitudes or decisions lead to spiritual numbness? How does a person begin to "feel" again?

2. In what ways does the church's hypocrisy reflect a suppression of God's Word? What sins have we in the church made "respectable"? What has been the response of the lost world around us?

3. What are some lies that our world believes in contrast to the truth of God revealed through creation? What are some lies that we in the church believe in contrast to the truth of God revealed in His Word?

4. In what ways is sin related to unbelief in the promises of God? Why might we prefer the word "mistakes" over "sin" when speaking of our attitudes and actions?

5. Is it possible to run from God while trying to earn His favor? How can our "best efforts" get in the way of true salvation?

6. How does our inability to save ourselves provide a platform for God to display His glory? How does "boasting in the gospel" influence the way we think about evangelism and missions?

7. What are some signs in a person's life that indicate God's work in preparing their heart for salvation? How can we discern these signs in order to share the gospel?

8. Are you more sensitive to God's Word and voice now than when you first believed?

9. How does our being healed of spiritual leprosy lead us to take the message of healing to the spiritual lepers around us?

Rather than trusting God's Word, we question it, belittle it, and disobey it.

God's moral standard reflects his character, guides all relationships and reveals our need for grace.

Our disobedience created a separation our actions can't repair and our desires can't overcome.

PART 3

CHRIST'S PERFECT RESPONSE TO GOD'S WORD

Fallen as we are, dead in our sin, we can never fix ourselves; we can never stand before the holy God—that is, apart from God's grace in Jesus Christ. According to God's will, Jesus became like us to take our place so we could share in His. Where we failed, He obeyed; where we confused, He clarified; where we defied, He submitted. Christ's response to God Word was perfect, and He gives the benefits of that response to us in faith.

Voices from the Church

"Where Adam and Eve had cringed in hiding when they heard the sound of God walking in the garden, this man stands, unashamed, before the voice of his Father. Where Israel had trembled in the desert in front of the glowing mountain, begging not to hear the voice of God (Ex. 20:19), Jesus stands, unafraid, before his Father's voice. Unlike them, bearing as they did the shame of the satanic curse, this man has nothing to hide. His Father is well pleased with him." [1]

—*Russell Moore*

CHAPTER 7
JESUS
The Faithful Son Who Obeys God's Word

AFFIRMED

Luke 3:21-22 *When all the people were baptized, Jesus also was baptized. As He was praying, heaven opened, and the Holy Spirit descended on Him in a physical appearance like a dove. And a voice came from heaven: You are My beloved Son. I take delight in You!*

IMAGINE THE SCENE THAT DAY. Jesus is making His way to the Jordan River where John the Baptist has been baptizing people. John spots Jesus approaching and declares, "Here is the Lamb of God, who takes away the sin of the world!" (John 1:29). The people must have been amazed at such a declaration.

However, their amazement is only heightened as Jesus enters the Jordan's waters and is baptized and God Himself declares, "You are My beloved Son. I take delight in You!" (Luke 3:22). This scene is amazing! There are many incredible things happening in this text. We see the Triune God on full display: the Son is being baptized, the Father declares His pleasure, and the Spirit descends to rest upon the Son. We also see the inauguration of Jesus' earthly ministry with this event. But perhaps the greatest thing we see in this text is God the Father's verbal affirmation of Jesus' qualifications to fulfill the righteous requirements that expected of us. This is great news for us.

Jesus was the unique Son of God. He was fully God and fully man. As fully God, He alone was able to come and be the sinless Savior for man. As fully man, He alone was able to pay the debt that humanity owed to God. When the time had come for Jesus to begin His earthly ministry, and make His first step toward the cross in Jerusalem, God the Father declares His approval of His Son's worthiness for the task. Because of this we rejoice! For as God is satisfied with His Son, He is also satisfied with all who are found with faith in His Son.

PAUSE AND REFLECT

▷ When your parents express their loving affirmation with you over something you have done, how does it make you feel?

▷ What lengths have you gone to in striving to win someone's affirmation? Was it worth what you had to do to earn it?

▷ Why do you think we all desire to be affirmed and liked, even by people we don't know?

TEMPTED YET SUCCESSFUL

Luke 4:1-13 *Then Jesus returned from the Jordan, full of the Holy Spirit, and was led by the Spirit in the wilderness for 40 days to be tempted by the Devil. He ate nothing during those days, and when they were over, He was hungry. The Devil said to Him, "If You are the Son of God, tell this stone to become bread." But Jesus answered him, "It is written: Man must not live on bread alone." So he took Him up and showed Him all the kingdoms of the world in a moment of time. The Devil said to Him, "I will give You their splendor and all this authority, because it has been given over to me, and I can give it to anyone I want. If You, then, will worship me, all will be Yours." And Jesus answered him, "It is written: Worship the Lord your God, and serve Him only." So he took Him to Jerusalem, had Him stand on the pinnacle of the temple, and said to Him, "If You are the Son of God, throw Yourself down from here. For it is written: He will give His angels orders concerning you, to protect you, and they will support you with their hands,so that you will not strike your foot against a stone." And Jesus answered him, "It is said: Do not test the Lord your God." After the Devil had finished every temptation, he departed from Him for a time.*

HAVE YOU EVER KNOWN SOMEONE who does everything well? There always seem to be one or two of them around us. These are the people who could dribble better, tackle harder, and run faster. They always made great grades, remembered everything, and studied less than everyone else. You know these types. They just seem to be one notch ahead of everyone else. Usually these people are not the objects of our affections. It isn't that they are good at things, it is usually their attitude about it that we dislike. If only their success in life was reflected in their attitude. In many ways, Jesus is just like these people. He is far superior in all his ways. Successful where we have failed. Victorious where we have lost. However, with Jesus, rather than responding with envy and jealously, we can respond with worship and adoration. His victories secure our victory. His successes become our successes, and erase our failures.

It is amazing to think about the sinlessness of Jesus. Because we are painfully aware of our sinfulness and imperfections, it gives us some insight into the magnificence of Jesus' perfection. Take a moment to take in this idea: in every way that we are tempted, Jesus was tempted, yet he never sinned (Heb. 4:15). He never once failed to obey His Father at every point of the Law. What an amazing Savior we have!

PAUSE AND REFLECT

▷ What does it mean to you that Christ's success and victories can be shared by you?

▷ If He was able to resist Satan's traps and temptations, and He is empowering you, do you have to give in to sin?

▷ What is one area of your life you are desperate for a victory today? Spend some time in prayer asking for God's help.

PROPHECIES FULFILLED

Luke 4:40-41 *When the sun was setting, all those who had anyone sick with various diseases brought them to Him. As He laid His hands on each one of them, He would heal them. Also, demons were coming out of many, shouting and saying, "You are the Son of God!" But He rebuked them and would not allow them to speak, because they knew He was the Messiah.*

HOW DO WE KNOW IF Jesus is the one who can save us? Is there a way to judge if Jesus was the expected Savior? To prove He was who He said He was?

Jesus anticipated and answered questions like these. On one occasion, Jesus went to his hometown of Nazareth on the Sabbath Day and went to the synagogue to preach. Upon arrival He is given a scroll of the prophet Isaiah. He opens it to Isaiah 61 and reads the first two verses and then declares to them, "Today as you listen, this Scripture has been fulfilled." (Luke 4:21).

What did he mean by this? He meant that He was the one doing the things that passage predicted the Messiah would do. He was the anointed proclaimer of Good News. He was the healer of the sick, blind, and lame. Jesus came to fulfill the Word of God. He came to do all that God's Holy Word commanded, and in doing so, He proved He was the One all history had been pointing to and waiting for.

What is the aim and intent of Jesus' fulfilling of the Word of God? To bring forth restoration to the fallen race of Adam and to make all things new (Rev. 21:5). Jesus came to bring forth the Kingdom of God. In the bringing forth of the kingdom, He is inaugurating a new reality.

When sin entered the Garden, creation became broken. He is reversing the effects of the fall, both in the descendants of Adam and the creation. His obedience to those written prophecies show that he alone has the authority to bring forth this new reality, and He expects us and enables us to take part in this new reality.

PAUSE AND REFLECT

▷ Do you truly believe Jesus is who He claimed to be?

▷ What difference does that belief make in your life?

▷ Are you actively taking part is God's restoration project?

▷ What is holding you back?

JESUS: THE FAITHFUL SON

Jesus is uniquely able to be our righteousness, succeed where we failed, and restore creation.

ACROSS COUNTRIES AND CULTURES, people from all walks of life sense deep down that this life is not all there is. If you were to poll your family and friends, you would find that regardless of their ethnicity or culture, most of them harbor a hope for a life beyond this one, a life of eternal peace and joy.

Throughout history, the "holy books" of other religions have offered ways by which a follower may enter into the next life. Islam, for example, teaches that if you follow the Five Pillars, you will enter paradise. Buddhism offers an eightfold path to nirvana (freedom from suffering). Regardless of the religion, the answer is the same: you must *do something* to become acceptable in order to enter the next world.

The problem with the solutions provided by other religions is that you can never know if you've done enough to become acceptable to enter the next life. Tim Keller writes: "Self-salvation through good works may produce a great deal of moral behavior in your life, but inside you are filled with self-righteousness, cruelty, and bigotry, and you are miserable. You are always comparing yourself to other people, and you are never sure you are being good enough. You cannot, therefore, deal with your hideousness and self-absorption through the moral law, by trying to be a good person through an act of the will. You need a complete transformation of the very motives of your heart."[1]

The gospel provides what the various religions of the world cannot—the kind of assurance of eternal life that transforms our hearts and lives. Every person in the world, including you and me, must face the question "What will it take to be acceptable to enter into eternal life?" The religions say there is work we must do. The gospel takes us back to a work that has been done.

Jesus is uniquely able to...

▶ BE OUR RIGHTEOUSNESS (LUKE 3:21-22).

21 When all the people were baptized, Jesus also was baptized. As He was praying, heaven opened, 22 and the Holy Spirit descended on Him in a physical appearance like a dove. And a voice came from heaven: You are My beloved Son. I take delight in You!

We all want to be accepted. Whether it's from our parents, friends at school, or even strangers, we all want to be accepted and affirmed. Why do you think we take so much time in making sure we look a certain way (fashion), talk a certain way (lingo, jargon), and behave a certain way (cultural etiquette)?

The desire to be accepted by others is a distortion of the desire God has placed in each of us to be accepted and affirmed by *Him*. The ultimate acceptance and affirmation we need comes from God. As we strive after other's acceptance, we are always left longing. We know deep in our bones that something is wrong with us. The Bible confirms that feeling of uneasiness, informing us that we are not acceptable to God because of our sin.

Though many sincere people follow the teachings of various religions in order to be accepted by God, the Bible tells us that our sin makes us unacceptable. One of the Scripture passages from last chapter's lesson told us "our best efforts to attain righteousness are in vain" (Isa. 64:6). If even our best deeds are in vain, is there any hope of being accepted and affirmed by God?

God has spoken to us in His Word and through creation. We have rejected His Word and chosen to go our own way. We need God to fix what we broke in order that we might be reconciled to Him.

The Bible gives us good news. We do not have to fear being rejected by God because God Himself has provided a way by which sinners may be accepted before Him. Luke, the evangelist, records the baptism of Jesus of Nazareth in order to show us that Jesus was uniquely qualified to provide the way for sinners to be accepted before God.

First, Jesus was uniquely qualified to bring us to God because He was the Lord's anointed, the Messiah-Christ. God had previously promised He would send a Servant who would carry our sorrows and bear our sins (Isa. 53:4-6). The Coming One would be anointed by the Holy Spirit to accomplish God's mission to seek and save the lost. Luke identifies Jesus as the promised anointed one (Christ) who came to liberate God's people from sin's slavery (Luke 4:16-21; see Isa. 61:1-2).

Second, Jesus was uniquely qualified to bring us to God because He was and is God's faithful Son, and the Father is pleased with His obedience (Luke 3:22). Jesus is the faithful and obedient Son who was empowered by the Holy Spirit to save God's people by fulfilling the righteousness God required in order to bring them to God. Though Jesus had never sinned, He identified with His sinful people by being baptized.

Here we see the distinction between religion and the gospel. Religion is about what you must do in order to be accepted before God; Christianity is about what God has done for you in order to accept you. As Tim Keller has said, "In religion, we try to obey the divine standards out of fear. We believe that if we don't obey we are going to lose God's blessing in this world and the next. In the gospel, the motivation is one of gratitude for the blessing we have already received because of Christ."[4]

This is the good news of the gospel—through faith in Christ, the Lord's anointed, we can be accepted before a holy God. And those whom God accepts He also empowers by His Holy Spirit for obedience and ministry!

▶ SUCCEED WHERE WE FAILED (LUKE 4:1-13).

[1] Then Jesus returned from the Jordan, full of the Holy Spirit, and was led by the Spirit in the wilderness [2] for [40] days to be tempted by the Devil. He ate nothing during those days, and when they were over, He was hungry.

[3] The Devil said to Him, "If You are the Son of God, tell this stone to become bread."[4] But Jesus answered him, "It is written: Man must not live on bread alone."

[5] So he took Him up and showed Him all the kingdoms of the world in a moment of time. [6] The Devil said to Him, "I will give You their splendor and all this authority, because it has been given over to me, and I can give it to anyone I want.

[7] If You, then, will worship me, all will be Yours."

[8] And Jesus answered him, "It is written: Worship the Lord your God, and serve Him only."

[9] So he took Him to Jerusalem, had Him stand on the pinnacle of the temple, and said to Him, "If You are the Son of God, throw Yourself down from here.

[10] For it is written: He will give His angels orders concerning you, to protect you, [11] and they will support you with their hands, so that you will not strike your foot against a stone." [12] And Jesus answered him, "It is said: Do not test the Lord your God."[13] After the Devil had finished every temptation, he departed from Him for a time.

When thinking of a substitute, we often think of a substitute teacher, which was never as good as the "real thing." Students generally treat the substitute with disrespect. After all, they have little authority because they have no part in establishing the lesson plan or exercising control over the students' grades.

Our experience of a classroom substitute is quite different than the Bible's presentation of Jesus as a substitute for sinful humanity. We think of a substitute as a temporary and poor replacement of the "real thing," but the Bible presents those who came before Jesus as the copies, or types, who pointed to Jesus who is the real thing.

Let's go back to the beginning and look at Adam as an example. Adam, the first man, represented us before God. God spoke His word to Adam, letting him know how to live as God's obedient son (Gen. 2:15-17). Unfortunately, Adam failed; he and Eve listened as the serpent questioned and distorted God's word, leading them to disobedience (3:1-8). Since he was our representative, when Adam sinned against God, we sinned with him, which made us guilty and unacceptable before a holy God (Rom. 5:12,18-19).

Even today, Satan is still up to his old tricks of distorting God's Word and deceiving us into thinking it says something other than what God has spoken. Consider the tragic incident of racism and slavery in American history. Professing Christians defended slavery on the basis that Africans were less than human. On those grounds, certain Christian theologians defended slavery, even claiming it would help evangelize the heathens!

The nation of Israel was also God's representative people, the descendants of Abraham through whom God would bless the world (Gen. 12:1-3). God made a promise to His people: "Now if you will listen to Me and carefully keep My covenant, you will be My own possession out of all the peoples, although all the earth is Mine, and you will be My kingdom of priests and My holy nation" (Ex. 19:5-6).

As God's treasured, firstborn son (4:22), Israel was to serve as God's priests, declaring God's name to the nations so that the world would know He alone is God. Yet just like Adam, Israel failed to obey God's Word. So God made them wander in the wilderness for 40 years (Num. 14:33-34).

The Gospels shine a spotlight on Jesus, the Messiah of Israel. He was the true representative and substitute for sinful humanity. Jesus faced the Devil as Adam did, and Jesus fought temptation in the wilderness, just like Israel. But unlike Adam and Israel, Jesus succeeded in the mission. He obeyed God at every point they failed. Jesus is the faithful Adam and the faithful Israel who obeyed God's Word.

Jesus responded to Satan's temptations by quoting Deuteronomy 8:3; 6:13,16. In these passages, Israel was preparing to cross the Jordan River and enter the promised land. By quoting from Deuteronomy, Jesus identified Himself with Israel. In other words, whereas Israel failed to obey God's Word as they prepared to cross the Jordan River, Jesus kept God's Word after crossing through the waters of baptism and fighting temptation— by trusting (and quoting!) the very word God had given to Israel.

Jesus is a faithful representative and substitute because He fulfilled all righteousness. He was obedient to God's Word at the exact point where Adam and Israel failed. That means Jesus is *our* faithful representative and substitute too. He has fulfilled all righteousness by being obedient to the Father where you and I have failed.

This is the good news of the gospel. The Father accepts Jesus' obedience on behalf of those who put their trust in Christ. We are unacceptable before a holy God, but Jesus is acceptable, and God affirms Jesus because He pleased the Father (Luke 3:22). By faith in Jesus Christ, we are acceptable to God and receive the same affirmation. The words the Father uttered over Jesus at His baptism ("You are My beloved Son. I take delight in You!") are true of us as well.

When you trust Jesus for your acceptance before a holy God, you are liberated from sin's slavery and curse. After all, this is what Jesus came to do—to restore what sin has destroyed.

▶ RESTORE CREATION (LUKE 4:40-41; CF. 4:16-21,31-39).

40 When the sun was setting, all those who had anyone sick with various diseases brought them to Him. As He laid His hands on each one of them, He would heal them. 41 Also, demons were coming out of many, shouting and saying, "You are the Son of God!" But He rebuked them and would not allow them to speak, because they knew He was the Messiah.

Because of sin, God's good creation has been infiltrated by all kinds of evil: disease, death, chaos, and poverty. Sin has tarnished God's good creation, leaving its awful effects all around us, including in our own bodies that waste away due to age and disease. The Bible goes so far as to say that we are enslaved to sin and its effects (Rom. 6:17-22).

As God's Messiah, Jesus not only fulfilled all righteousness by identifying with humanity and obeying where we've failed, but He also announced the good news of God's kingdom (Luke 4:42-44). Jesus' arrival marked the beginning of the kingdom of God, the rule of God where the effects of sin on creation were to be halted and reversed and God's people were to be liberated from sin's hold on them.

Since Jesus was the Messiah, anointed by God's Spirit to accomplish God's mission, Jesus had authority over all creation (5:1-10; 8:22-25). Jesus displayed this authority when He liberated people from physical bondage by healing their diseases (4:38-40) and from spiritual bondage by casting out their demons (vv. 41-44).

B. B. Warfield, the famous Princeton theologian, described Christ's work this way: "When our Lord came down to earth He drew heaven with Him. The signs which accompanied His ministry were but the trailing clouds of glory which He brought from heaven, which is His home. The number of the miracles which He wrought may easily be underrated. It has been said that in effect He banished disease and death from Palestine for the three years of His ministry."[9]

▶ THE ALREADY/NOT YET NATURE OF GOD'S KINGDOM

Jesus' healings and exorcisms were not only proof of His authority as God's Messiah, they were also a foretaste of the future arrival of God's kingdom in its fullness when there would be no more disease and no more evil. The fact that we still experience sickness and evil today, including demon possession, indicates that though Jesus inaugurated the kingdom of God at His first coming, it has not fully arrived. Though there is a sense that in Jesus the kingdom is already here, until Jesus comes again, the kingdom will not yet fully arrive. Only when Jesus returns will there be no more pain, sorrow, disease, death, chaos, or evil (Rev. 21:1-4).

Ed Stetzer uses a popular illustration to describe the "already" and "not yet" nature of God's kingdom. "As World War II came to a close, there were two important dates. The first one occurred on June 6, 1944. History remembers it as 'D-day.' As a part of Operation Overlord, the United States and its allies landed on the beach of Normandy, France. It was the beginning of the end of the war. Yet the war in Europe didn't end until more than a year later on May 7, 1945, also known as 'VE-day.' Despite the fact that the victory at Normandy effectively broke the back of the Axis powers, the war didn't officially end until months later. In fact, more people died in between those dates than any other period of the war. It was dark and difficult, but the end had begun. It was inaugurated June 6, 1944, but the end wasn't consummated until May 7, 1945. That's the difference between D-day and VE-day. That's not a perfect parallel, but when the kingdom of God arrived in the person of Jesus, it came near. But, it will not be fully realized until Jesus returns at the end of time. The church is left to live between the times."[11]

Until the day of Christ's return, those who have put their trust in Jesus Christ and have stopped trusting in their own works for acceptance before God live with the confident hope that we are accepted before God because of Jesus' righteousness. Even though we may still fail to obey and fall into sin, we receive God's forgiveness granted to us through Christ's obedience to God's Word.

As we await the return of Christ, the Father is placing every enemy under Jesus' feet (Eph. 1:22). After Jesus has defeated all His enemies, including death, He will deliver the kingdom to the Father, and we will enter into God's final rest, where we will finally be free from sin and disease and death (1 Cor. 15:24-28).

▶ CONCLUSION

Jesus fulfilled the righteousness God requires of humanity by identifying with God's previous sinful human representatives (Adam and Israel) and reenacting their lives at the very points they failed. Christ's obedience began to reverse the effects of sin unleashed upon God's people and the created world. Jesus was uniquely qualified to fulfill God's mission because He was the Lord's anointed, the Messiah-Christ.

As those who are accepted by God through Christ, we too have been empowered by the Holy Spirit for mission and ministry. The Bible declares that we are "a chosen race, a royal priesthood, a holy nation, a people for His possession" (1 Pet. 2:9). In other words, though in and of ourselves we are unacceptable to God, in Christ we are not only acceptable to God but God affirms us, calling us His sons and daughters and sending us out to accomplish His mission—to "proclaim the praises of the One who called you out of darkness into His marvelous light."

Now Jesus is working through us, in the power of the Holy Spirit, to continue telling the world that He alone is God and the only pathway to the Father. As we proclaim this good news of God's kingdom, we will see people liberated from bondage to sin.

QUESTIONS

1. Have you ever considered how many of your actions and desires are impacted by seeking the affirmation and acceptance of others? Where are you most motivated by others' acceptance and affirmation? What are some things you do that is motivated by affirmation?

2. How do people try to overcome the fear of not measuring up to God's standard? To the standard of people around them?

3. Do you struggle with believing the Father has accepted you in Christ? How does understanding the message of Christianity, the gospel, liberate people from bondage to sin?

4. In our individualist society, it is difficult for people to understand how one person's sin can affect other people. Why is it important that we maintain the biblical teaching that Adam's sin is passed down to us? What evidence of this do we see in our own lives?

5. Can you think of other examples when God's Word has been misused to justify sin? Have you ever been confused about God's Word and what God desires of us? How did the Holy Spirit correct your false thinking?

6. What Old Testament book did Jesus quote from? What is the context of the verses Jesus quoted, and what do you think His quotes indicated for people in His day? What does that teach us about fighting sin and temptation?

7. To what do unbelieving people attribute all the evil, chaos, and disorder in our world? What does the Bible say is the source of the evil in our world? What do unbelievers think will put an end to the chaos and evil around us? What does the Bible say will put an end to the chaos and evil around us?

8. Can you imagine what a world free from the effects of sin would be like? What must it have been like to experience Christ's miracles first hand? Is that any different than reading about them today?

9. How does a future hope of being in God's presence where there is no sin, suffering, sorrow, and death help you face sin, suffering, sorrow, and death now?

10. How does a future hope of no sickness or suffering influence our mission as Christ's representatives in the world?

CHAPTER 8

JESUS

The Faithful Teacher Who Explains and Fulfills God's Word

THE GREAT INTERPRETER

Matt. 5:17 *"Don't assume that I came to destroy the Law or the Prophets. I did not come to destroy but to fulfill."*

I RECENTLY WENT ON A mission trip to Haiti. In Haiti, Creole and French are the dominant languages. English, my dominant and secondary language, is not spoken by many of the native Haitians. Right away, I knew this was going to be a difficulty we would have to deal with.

On this trip I was with several pastors and we were working with multiple indigenous Haitian churches. We taught a pastor's conference, a youth conference, and worshiped in their churches on Sunday morning. It was amazing being able to worship alongside these believers, but the language barrier kept presenting problems.

One of our main issues became the lack of interpreters. We had plenty of English Bible teachers and plenty of Haitian churches to teach in, but we did not have enough translators. Having someone to interpret, and interpret correctly, is very important in communication. With matters as weighty as salvation and the things of God, you do not want something you say to be interpreted incorrectly and since I didn't know any Creole and very little French, having a trusted interpreter was essential.

When you begin to think about how important this is, take into consideration the importance of Jesus coming to us to teach us what the Old Testament is really about. Think about how incapable we are of knowing the way of the kingdom of God without Jesus. He perfectly interpreted to us things known only in the wisdom of God and made them available to us. He showed things to us only discernible by the Spirit of God, and then gave us His Spirit to keep guiding us into these truths (John 16:13). He was not only the perfect teacher but also the perfect interpreter.

What a perfect and matchless Savior we have in Christ, our Great Interpreter of the truths of God!

PAUSE AND REFLECT

▷ What qualities does an interpreter need to possess? How was Christ the perfect interpreter?

▷ How does the right understanding change everything?

▷ Have you ever been in a situation where you thought something was true only to find out you didn't understand it correctly?

THE HEART BEHIND THE ACTIONS

Matt. 5:21-22, 27-28 *"You have heard that it was said to our ancestors, Do not murder, and whoever murders will be subject to judgment. But I tell you, everyone who is angry with his brother will be subject to judgment. And whoever says to his brother, 'Fool!' will be subject to the Sanhedrin. But whoever says, 'You moron!' will be subject to hellfire."*

HAVE YOU EVER WITNESSED SOMEONE doing the right thing with the wrong motives? It happens all the time—people serving and helping others, not because of their sincere desire to help, but out of their sincere desire to be praised for helping.

There are people who attempt to do the right things morally, not because they seek to honor God, but because they seek relief from guilt or public shame. In these cases, it is evident that someone may be doing the right things, but with the wrong motives. Is it possible to do the right things, but still have a corrupt heart? God does not seek people who look only to do the right things, He searches the heart of man when judging our actions.

While teaching during his Sermon on the Mount, Jesus explains this reality to the onlookers and listeners. Jesus teaches about the laws they had grown accustomed to hearing, but He immediately surprises everyone by raising the bar on those laws. He reminds them that it is not enough to avoid murder, but our hearts should be such that we avoid hatred. It is not enough that we resist adultery, but our hearts should be such that we resist lust.

The issue is not about the external sin being avoided, but about the internal workings of the heart behind the sin. It is not enough to do good or right things: Jesus teaches us to interpret the law by showing the heart behind it.

PAUSE AND REFLECT

▷ **Describe a time when you did the right thing but for the wrong reasons?**

▷ **What was the result of those actions?**

▷ **Which rules do you easily obey by focusing on the rule and not the intent?**

EXPECTATIONS SET AND MET

Matt. 5:43-48 *"You have heard that it was said, Love your neighbor and hate your enemy. But I tell you, love your enemies and pray for those who persecute you, so that you may be sons of your Father in heaven. For He causes His sun to rise on the evil and the good, and sends rain on the righteous and the unrighteous. For if you love those who love you, what reward will you have? Don't even the tax collectors do the same? And if you greet only your brothers, what are you doing out of the ordinary? Don't even the Gentiles do the same? Be perfect, therefore, as your heavenly Father is perfect."*

I REMEMBER GROWING UP PLAYING sports, and even in the Army as a soldier, times when a coach or superior officer would command me to do something that they themselves could not do. Have you ever experienced this? A coach tells you to run five laps around the field, but you know he could not manage one lap without needing oxygen. A parent requires you to clean your bedroom when theirs would qualify to be featured on an episode of "Hoarders." These situations bother us so much because there is a part of us that expects the people giving the commands and making the rules to be doing the things they are dictating. This just makes sense right?

Thankfully, Jesus does not fall into this category. He taught us the loftiest of truths. He raised the bar to highest levels. He revealed to us the mysteries of the kingdom of God hidden from eternity's past (Matt. 13:11). These are the biggest, most gigantic truths in all the world.

However, He never commanded or laid out one expectation of God that He Himself did not meet and fulfill. This is the amazing thing about Jesus. He not only came to teach us what the Kingdom of God was like and what citizens of this kingdom were supposed to live like, but He came to model it and fulfill those requirements at the same time. When He met God's expectations, He did so for us. In our place. He did this not only because he was the perfect Savior, but because he was the Master Teacher. As our great teacher, he modeled with his life the very things he taught us with His words.

PAUSE AND REFLECT

▷ How do you respond when someone commands something they either don't do or can't do?

▷ Would you hire a badly out-of-shape person to be your personal trainer? Why or why not?

▷ How does knowing Christ has both set and met God's standards in your place impact your life?

JESUS: THE FAITHFUL TEACHER

Jesus fulfills the law by rightly interpreting it, revealing the true intent, and meeting God's expectations.

DO YOU FIND the Old Testament hard to understand (and sometimes hard to believe)? Are there parts of the Old Testament that make you cringe? If so, you're not alone. A good number of people today openly question the validity and value of the Old Testament. Some even go so far as to question the reality of the Old Testament God.

In his book *The God Delusion*, evolutionary biologist Richard Dawkins emphatically states: "The God of the Old Testament is arguably the most unpleasant character in all fiction: jealous and proud of it; a petty, unjust, unforgiving control-freak; a vindictive, bloodthirsty ethnic cleanser; a misogynistic, homophobic, racist, infanticidal, genocidal, filicidal, pestilential, megalomaniacal, sadomasochistic, capriciously malevolent bully."[1] Talk about a litany of negative characteristics! (In case you couldn't tell from reading this quote, Dawkins is an avowed atheist.)

Throughout church history, there have been those who have registered their distaste for the Old Testament and the law-giving God portrayed there. The most famous was Marcion, son of the bishop of Sinope in Pontus around A.D. 144. Marcion believed that Jesus' teaching contradicted the Old Testament. In his view, the Old Testament god (Yahweh) was vindictive and evil, while the New Testament God (the Father) was loving and gracious in sending Jesus into the world as Savior. So Marcion rejected the Old Testament and proposed a list of books that should be considered as authoritative for the church. His list included only those New Testament books that allowed him to maintain his pitting of Jesus against the Old Testament. (In the end, all he was left with was a mangled version of Luke's Gospel and a handful of chopped up letters from Paul.)

Christians rightly rejected the views of Marcion. Even today, we recoil at Marcion's teachings. But even if we would never think of ourselves as modern-day Marcionites, might it be possible that our approach to the Old Testament sometimes resembles Marcion's in practice? Let's consider some diagnostic questions:

- Do we value the Old Testament?
- Do we read and meditate on it?
- Do we seek to apply it to our lives?

- Do we gravitate primarily (or even solely) to the New Testament in our Bible reading and study?
- Do we reduce the Old Testament to little more than illustrative material for the New?

These questions can help us discern a faulty view of the Old Testament. Why does this matter? Because, as the quote from Richard Dawkins illustrates so well, one's view of the Bible and one's view of God go hand in hand.

Jesus Fulfills the Law by...

▶ RIGHTLY INTERPRETING IT (MATT. 5:17).

17 "Don't assume that I came to destroy the Law or the Prophets. I did not come to destroy but to fulfill."

It's not difficult to see why someone might assume that Jesus came to destroy the Old Testament. After all, Jesus taught that His coming signified a new era, one that marked the end of certain Old Testament commands and institutions, such as food laws (Mark 7:19), the temple (Matt. 24:1-2), and the entire sacrificial system (Heb. 8:13; 10:1-18).

Contrary to the assumption that Jesus came to destroy the Old Testament, Jesus declared that His teaching was in complete harmony with it—all of it. In fact, Jesus said that not even the smallest, seemingly inconsequential parts of the words of the law would pass away "until all things are accomplished" (Matt. 5:18).

The Law and the Prophets pointed to a future time when all of its commands, promises, and institutions would be fulfilled. With Jesus' coming, the time of fulfillment had arrived. That is why Jesus explained His mission in relation to the Old Testament—"I [came] to fulfill" (v. 17). Jesus fulfilled the Law and the Prophets because they pointed to Him.

The right way to interpret the Old Testament is by following Jesus' lead in seeing how it is all about Him!
- Jesus is the true and faithful Israel whom God called out of Egypt (2:15) and who did not put the Lord to the test during His wilderness wandering (4:1-11).
- Jesus is the new temple who fulfills the old one that was destroyed (John 2:18-22).
- Jesus is the real bread from heaven (manna) giving life to the world (6:30-35).
- Jesus is the Lamb of God who takes away the sin of the world (1:29).

With unique authority, Jesus taught that we cannot understand the Old Testament apart from Him; He is the interpretive lens through which we must understand the Hebrew Scriptures. This means that Jesus was faithful to teach God's Word precisely because He explained God's Word in light of Himself. Only Jesus could provide the faithful and true interpretation of God's Word.

▶ SIX QUESTIONS TO ASK OF GOD'S WORD

Seeing Jesus at the center of the Scriptures helps us to rightly interpret God's Word today. J. I. Packer lists six questions that we should ask of the biblical text we are studying in order to be faithful interpreters. Use these questions when you are seeking to understand God's Word:

1. What do these words actually mean?
2. What light do other Scriptures throw on this text? Where and how does it fit into the total biblical revelation?
3. What truths does it teach about God, and about man in relation to God?
4. How are these truths related to the saving work of Christ, and what light does the gospel of Christ throw upon them?
5. What experiences do these truths delineate, or explain, or seek to create or cure? For what practical purpose do they stand in Scripture?
6. How do they apply to myself and others in our own actual situation? To what present human condition do they speak, and what are they telling us to believe and do? [4]

▶ REVEALING THE TRUE INTENT (MATT. 5:21-22,27-28).

Imagine that a friend of yours found out you liked a particular girl at school. Embarrassed, you make him promise not to tell her how you feel. The next day at school everyone is talking about you wanting to ask out your secret crush. This causes all kinds of problems for you because now you feel awkward being around her and you have several classes with her. As you confront your "friend," he replies, "You said not to tell her, I didn't." Frustrated, you say, "That wasn't the point. I didn't want her to know, and now she does." Technically your friend obeyed your command to not tell her, but by telling everyone else, she found out. He obeyed the letter of the law without understanding the true intent.

There are all sorts of ways to obey the letter of the law and miss its intention. It's easy to become so focused on the rules and regulations that we miss the point of them. We need the law-giver to remind us of the law's intention to push us back to the heart of the matter.

As the One to whom the Law and the Prophets pointed, Jesus was the faithful interpreter of God's Word. The scribes and Pharisees followed an oral tradition that represented a moralistic interpretation of the law. They were all about the letter of the law, but they had missed the heart.

Jesus, on the other hand, explained the true meaning of the law as God intended. Contrary to what the people had heard, Jesus declared that the intention of the law was not about checking off a list of moral requirements but total obedience that flowed from a pure heart. Anything less excludes one from the kingdom of heaven. Consider just two examples of Jesus' teaching in relation to God's law.

21 "You have heard that it was said to our ancestors, Do not murder, and whoever murders will be subject to judgment. 22 But I tell you, everyone who is angry with his brother will be subject to judgment. And whoever says to his brother, 'Fool!' will be subject to the Sanhedrin. But whoever says, 'You moron!' will be subject to hellfire."

The phrase "You have heard that it was said…But I tell you…" distinguished Jesus' teaching from that of the scribes and Pharisees and established Jesus as the authoritative interpreter of God's Word. Can you imagine a Christian preacher standing before a congregation and saying, "You've heard Jesus say this, *but I tell you…*"? If you were to hear such a thing, you'd march up to that pastor and ask, "Who do you think you are?" And that's the point. Jesus wasn't just revealing the true interpretation of God's law. He was also revealing His authority to say so.

Now back to Jesus' interpretation of the law regarding murder. Clearly the Sixth Commandment declared murder to be against the will of God (Ex. 20:13). We learn in Genesis that the reason murder is forbidden is because humankind is created in God's image (Gen. 1:26-28; 5:1-2); therefore, anyone who kills another human being created in God's image forfeits their own life (9:6).

Unlike the scribes and Pharisees, however, Jesus was not concerned merely with the physical act of murder; He was concerned with the sin of the heart that leads to murder—unrighteous anger. Jesus was not denying that murderers will be judged; that is the law. Jesus was simply saying that murder flows from a sinful heart, and sinners will be judged not only for their sinful actions but also for their sinful attitudes.

This may sound harsh to us, but it's actually the expression of our Savior's compassionate heart. Why the tough words? Because murder flows from an angry heart. If you don't believe that's true, consider Cain and Abel. God exposed Cain's anger (Gen. 4:6). It was Cain's anger that led him to kill Abel (4:8; see also 1 John 3:11-12). Murder begins in the heart.

There are many ways that murderous anger can slowly kill a soul. We murder people by destroying their reputations. We murder people, by how we speak to them. Such angry people, says Jesus, will be guilty at the judgment and experience the fire of hell rather than the eternal kingdom (Matt. 5:22).

We've spent a lot of time on the Sixth Commandment above because it is a common struggle for most of us, but we can apply Jesus' teaching to every area of our lives in light of God's law. Let's consider lust.

[27] *"You have heard that it was said, Do not commit adultery.* [28] *But I tell you, everyone who looks at a woman to lust for her has already committed adultery with her in his heart."*

We live in a sex-crazed world where sex sells (billboards, magazine ads, commercials, you name it…). It seems like every show on TV depicts all students as already having sex. It has become so common place in our culture, we run the risk of believing it ourselves. Sex is still designed to be between one man and one woman with in the bounds of a marriage relationship. Even for those that follow Christ, not having sex is not enough. There are ways we try to obey the law yet completely miss the intent, especially in this area.

The religious leaders of Jesus' day thought they were fulfilling the Seventh Commandment simply by avoiding sexual relations with someone who was not their spouse. But Jesus was interested in the heart attitudes that lead to the sinful physical act. The Pharisees seemed to have forgotten the Tenth Commandment: "Do not covet your neighbor's wife" (Ex. 20:17).

In His teaching, Jesus exposes the corruption of the human heart, the seriousness of sin, and the certainty of punishment for lawbreakers. Clearly, when we understand the law as God intended it, we are all shown to be lawbreakers. Jesus taught that we must deal with sin seriously because those who continue in unrepentant sin will be excluded from the kingdom of heaven and experience the fires of hell (Matt. 5:29-30; 7:21-23). Thankfully, this word of judgment leads to the offer of salvation.

▶ MEETING GOD'S EXPECTATIONS (MATT. 5:43-48).

Have you ever been to a theme park? Having moved to Florida as a kid, I grew up going to Disney World's Magic Kingdom. When the park closes in the evening, officials don't check to see if you had a ticket that allowed you to get in. Their main concern is that everyone get *out*! So they open all their gates and unlock all their turnstiles in order to guide their guests out of the park in an organized but speedy manner.

Entrance into the park is a completely different situation. If you want to get into the Magic Kingdom, you must show your ticket (proving that you paid the price of admission) and enter into the park individually through the turnstiles that are guarded by security. No ticket, no entrance.

At stake in Jesus' teaching is entrance into a kingdom. But we're not talking about some temporary escape into a fantastical, magical theme park. No, this is about everlasting inclusion in the kingdom of God where righteousness dwells.

Jesus accused the scribes and Pharisees of locking people out of God's kingdom (Matt. 23:13). The Pharisees had separated God's law from God's character, leading them to reduce the law to a set of moral rules that were to be followed in legalistic fashion. The idea was that by keeping the rules one could gain entrance into the kingdom.

Jesus could not have disagreed more (7:21-23). Instead, Jesus declared that "unless your righteousness surpasses that of the scribes and Pharisees, you will never enter the kingdom of heaven" (5:20).

Not only did Jesus correctly interpret the law, He also intensified it. How good is good enough? Total perfection.

[43] "You have heard that it was said, Love your neighbor and hate your enemy. [44] But I tell you, love your enemies and pray for those who persecute you, [45] so that you may be sons of your Father in heaven. For He causes His sun to rise on the evil and the good, and sends rain on the righteous and the unrighteous. [46] For if you love those who love you, what reward will you have? Don't even the tax collectors do the same? [47] And if you greet only your brothers, what are you doing out of the ordinary? Don't even the Gentiles do the same? [48] Be perfect, therefore, as your heavenly Father is perfect."

Did you catch that last verse? The standard of righteousness that God requires is perfection. None of us can meet that standard. God's law reveals the perfect character of God, and perfection is precisely what God expects of us. The problem is that we have all broken God's law. This is the great human dilemma.

The good news of the gospel is that Jesus came to fulfill the law. It was Jesus who loved His enemies fully, even praying for those who tormented Him on the cross. It was Jesus who welcomed tax collectors and sinners to His table. It was Jesus was showed us the perfection of the Father.

The law has two basic demands. First, the law demands perfect obedience that flows from a pure heart. Because our hearts are corrupt, we cannot fulfill this demand. Jesus, however, could and did by obeying the law at every point; He did not leave out even the smallest, seemingly insignificant parts of the words of the law.

Second, the law also demands the death penalty for lawbreakers. The good news is that Jesus fulfilled this demand by taking upon Himself the curse of the law on our behalf. The death penalty for lawbreaking was administered to Jesus on the cross.

Those who gain entrance into the kingdom of heaven, then, are not those who try to work at it but those who trust in Jesus' fulfilling of the law in their place. And those who truly believe will obey Jesus' teaching.

Through faith we are enabled to begin living in accordance with Jesus' teaching! As the apostle Paul declares, "the righteous will live by faith" (Gal. 3:11). This is the righteousness that surpasses that of the Pharisees.

▶ CONCLUSION

The Sermon on the Mount pushes us to the end of ourselves by exposing the corruption of our sinful hearts. When we recognize that Jesus fulfilled the demands of the law perfectly on our behalf, we are transformed. By faith in Jesus, the righteousness of Christ is accounted to us, and the penalty for our breaking the law is accounted to Christ. This is the great exchange!

Even better, by faith in Christ, we receive new hearts that allow us to obey all that Jesus taught—to love the Lord our God with every fiber of our being and to love our neighbor as ourselves. This too is a fulfillment of the Law and the Prophets (Jer. 31:31-34; Ezek. 36:24-27).

Now our mission is defined in relation to Jesus' teaching. Since Jesus faithfully fulfilled the Law and the Prophets, the Father has granted Him authority over heaven and earth. As the sovereign King, Jesus commands us to go out under His authority into the world with this good news. Our commission is not simply to baptize but to make disciples by also "teaching them to observe everything" that Jesus commanded (Matt. 28:18-20). Let us therefore embrace Jesus' teaching and tell others what He has taught us.

QUESTIONS

1. What negative images of the God of the Old Testament do you or the people around you have? How might negative views of God affect a person's desire to read and study the Old Testament?

2. What are some other Old Testament commands or institutions Jesus set aside? Think of some stories when Jesus acted in a way that challenged the prevailing understanding of the law in His day (see Matt. 9:1-8,14-15; 12:1-13).

3. How does understanding the Old Testament was pointing to Christ change your perspective on reading the Old Testament?

4. Describe a time when you obeyed the letter of the law but purposefully disobeyed the intent? How did your parents respond when you did this? Why is it important that we understand God's intentions when we seek to apply the Scriptures? How have you attempted to obey God's laws without obeying His intent?

5. Examine your heart. Are you harboring bitter thoughts toward people right now? Have you been angry with someone and not taken steps to reconcile? Have you ever associated these thoughts with murder?

6. What sins do you struggle with? How are you fighting against sin and temptation? How do these struggles with sin affect your understanding of whether or not you will enter the kingdom of heaven?

7. Since the scribes and the Pharisees were famous for keeping "the law," how could anyone's righteousness surpass theirs? Just what kind of righteousness does God's law require, or in today's terms, "How good is good enough?"

8. How does trusting in Christ's fulfilling work encourage you to have assurance of salvation? How would you explain the good news of the gospel in terms of Jesus fulfilling the Law and the Prophets to someone who has never heard it before? To someone who is struggling with assurance of salvation?

CHAPTER 9

JESUS

The Faithful Servant Who Submits to God's Word

VOLUNTEER WORK

Mark 14:32-36 *"Then they came to a place named Gethsemane, and He told His disciples, "Sit here while I pray." He took Peter, James, and John with Him, and He began to be deeply distressed and horrified. Then He said to them, "My soul is swallowed up in sorrow—to the point of death. Remain here and stay awake." Then He went a little farther, fell to the ground, and began to pray that if it were possible, the hour might pass from Him. And He said, "Abba, Father! All things are possible for You. Take this cup away from Me. Nevertheless, not what I will, but what You will."*

NOBODY VOLUNTEERS FOR SUFFERING. WE do not like hurt or pain very much. Typically most of us avoid pain at all cost. Generally, the only sufferings that most of us endure are the sufferings thrust upon us, usually leaving us without an option to face them. You may have been forced to face hurt or pain unwillingly because of a divorce, breakup, death in the family, a friend letting you down, or countless other ways, but volunteering for suffering? Most never have or will. But praise be to God, Jesus did.

Jesus Christ, our Savior, willingly suffered for us. He willingly endured the suffering of the cross, knowing the physical pain that would accompany it and knowing the separation and wrath coming from his Father in heaven. If anyone has ever been undeserving of suffering, it was the Lord Jesus. Yet he suffered voluntarily. With his death looming over Him in the Garden of Gethsemane, He prayed for the Father to remove the cup of suffering if possible. But ultimately, His desire was for his Father's will to be done, even if it meant His own suffering. His suffering brought us life and redeemed us. Jesus laid down his life to the Father's will.

If we belong to Christ, we too should willingly lay down our lives to God's will, even if suffering follows. Jesus warns that suffering will come to those who belong to Him (Matt. 10:22). Knowing this, we should still willingly submit our will to God. Christ has shown us the way.

PAUSE AND REFLECT

▷ When you think about "suffering" and your life, what comes to mind?

▷ Why was it important that Jesus endure suffering on our behalf?

▷ Jesus warns that suffering will come to those who belong to Him.

▷ What might that mean for your life?

SHAME EMBRACED

Phil. 2: 5-11 *"Make your own attitude that of Christ Jesus, who, existing in the form of God, did not consider equality with God as something to be used for His own advantage. Instead He emptied Himself by assuming the form of a slave, taking on the likeness of men. And when He had come as a man in His external form, He humbled Himself by becoming obedient to the point of death—even to death on a cross. For this reason God highly exalted Him and gave Him the name that is above every name, so that at the name of Jesus every knee should bow—of those who are in heaven and on earth and under the earth— and every tongue should confess that Jesus Christ is Lord, to the glory of God the Father.*

HAVE YOU EVER EXPERIENCED PUBLIC shame? There are all sorts of ways it can happen. It can happen accidentally through some circumstance like slipping and falling in the middle of the hallway between classes, or dropping an easy fly ball in a baseball game. It can also happen intentionally, as someone uses shame to embarrass and hurt you. Teachers may do this by making you stand up in class because you got caught talking as they were teaching. A coach may make you drop and do push-ups in front of the team because you messed up the play. Public shame can be a form of punishment.

Public shame is one the ways the Romans of Jesus' day would punish people. The use of crucifixion was simultaneously a form of physical punishment and shame. It brought shame on the person in multiple ways: they were naked and they were put on public display. With Jesus, they not only did this, but they brutally beat him, mocked him by placing a crown of thorns around his head, and placing a sign above him that read "King of the Jews." Jesus Christ our Lord became obedient to the point of death, even death on a cross. He humbled himself by taking on flesh, marching to the cross, despising its shame.

Why did Jesus embrace this shame? To accomplish the Father's grand design in salvation. Through his willingness to suffer pain and public humiliation, he became the propitiation (wrath-diverting sacrifice) for our sins. He did the work of redemption for us that we could never do for ourselves. In this way, he submitted to the Father's will, embracing the humiliation and shame.

PAUSE AND REFLECT

▷ **What public shame have you endured before? How does it make you feel to look back on it?**

▷ **How is shame related to suffering? Why would God allow Jesus to be exposed to both?**

WORTHY

Heb. 1:1-4 *"Long ago God spoke to the fathers by the prophets at different times and in different ways. In these last days, He has spoken to us by His Son. God has appointed Him heir of all things and made the universe through Him. The Son is the radiance of God's glory and the exact expression of His nature, sustaining all things by His powerful word. After making purification for sins, He sat down at the right hand of the Majesty on high. So He became higher in rank than the angels, just as the name He inherited is superior to theirs."*

THE BEST MOVIES IN THE world, I think, are the ones that end with the hero making some great sacrifice to save the lives of many people. In making the sacrifice, the people are saved and the individual is exalted as the great hero. I watched the movie *Armageddon* (1998) as a teenager. The story depicted a veteran astronaut and his team who are going to save the planet by diverting an oncoming asteroid from hitting Earth. This astronaut, Harry, is put in position where either he or his daughter's love interest, A.J., are going to have to stay behind and die to successfully accomplish the mission. A.J. appears to be the one tasked to do it, but at the last moment, Harry steps in, pushes A.J. aside, and takes his place. Harry destroys the asteroid and loses his life, but saves the planet and the man his daughter loves. The movie ends with Harry's funeral where he is honored and recognized as the great hero.

We love movies like this. Why is it that we love these types of stories and movies? Because deep down inside of us we know that we are in need of a rescue and we know the one who does it is worthy of all praise. The story of the gospel is one in which Jesus Christ willingly submitted his own life, in order to save a people for himself. Jesus willingly took our place, by taking on flesh and dying on the cross. On the third day he rose from the grave, conquering Satan, sin, and death. In doing so, He is exalted. He is the hero. He is worthy of worship, praise, and adoration. He is given the name that is above every name. After making purification for our sins, he was seated at the right hand of his Father. Jesus is the great hero.

PAUSE AND REFLECT

▷ **What movie can you think of that involves a hero sacrificing himself to take someone's place?**

▷ **What traits are common among those heroes?**

▷ **Does it change your view of the gospel to think of yourself as someone needing rescue, and Christ as the hero?**

JESUS: THE FAITHFUL SERVANT

When Christ submitted to the Father's Will, it brought great suffering, caused great shame, but lead to His exaltation.

"WHAT WOULD JESUS DO?" Do you remember the WWJD bracelets made popular in the 1990s? They were the rage for a while. No good Christian student was caught without one on their wrist. Eventually, they became so popular and mainstream, they lost their attractiveness to those truly trying to live out the initials. Did you know the phrase was actually made popular by Charles Sheldon's classic book In His Steps, first published in 1897.

Sheldon's fictional story begins as Reverend Henry Maxwell, pastor of First Church of Raymond, seeks the quiet solitude of his study at home in order to prepare Sunday's sermon on 1 Peter 2:21: "For you were called to this, because Christ also suffered for you, leaving you an example, so that you should follow in His steps." Maxwell is interrupted when a young man in his early thirties, disheveled, dirty, and homeless comes to his door. Anxious to return to his study, the pastor offers little help and wishes him well.

Much to Reverend Maxwell's surprise, the same homeless man stands up to speak to the congregation at the end of the sermon Maxwell had just finished on imitating Christ. He asks: "I was wondering, as I sat there under the gallery, if what you call following Jesus is the same thing as what He taught. What did He mean when He said, 'Follow Me'? The minister said that it was necessary for the disciple of Jesus to follow His steps, and he said the steps were obedience, faith, love, and imitation. But I did not hear him tell you just what he meant that to mean, especially the last step. What do Christians mean by following the steps of Jesus?"

While still speaking, the young man falls to the floor. Reverend Maxwell and his wife take him into their home to care for him, but he dies a few days later. Moved by this experience, Maxwell steps into the pulpit on the following Sunday and challenges the congregation: "Our motto will be, 'What would Jesus do?' Our aim will be to act just as He would if He were in our places, regardless of immediate results. In other words, we propose to follow Jesus' steps as closely and as literally as we believe He taught His disciples to do. And those who volunteer to do this will pledge themselves for an entire year, beginning with to-day, so to act."[1]

Have you ever thought of this? Have you ever looked at your actions and truly tried to respond in a way that you think Christ would? What about the decisions you make would have to change? While this way of thinking has its benefits, it still doesn't get us to the proper place. The conclusion Maxwell arrived at is a worthy venture and the idea of asking what Jesus would do is good, but too often Christians apply this "imitation of Christ" only to ethical situations. The unintended result is that Jesus gets reduced to just a teacher of morals. Of course, it *is* true that we are called to imitate Christ. But too often, we don't think carefully about what this imitation looks like and what it will cost us.

Imitation of Christ requires meditation on Christ. If we are to know what it means to follow Christ, then we must seek to study Christ—His life and teaching and, most importantly, His death and resurrection. Therefore, if we are to imitate Christ, we need to begin with a different question—not just "What would Jesus do?" but "What has Jesus *done*?" Once we understand what Jesus has done, we can best understand how to represent Him and follow Him faithfully.

When Christ Submitted to the Father's Will...

▶ **IT BROUGHT GREAT SUFFERING (MARK 14:32-36).**

For many people today, "submission" is a dirty word. Our revulsion against submission is rooted in the sinful disposition we inherited from Adam that inclines us to rebel against authority. When Adam sinned, he essentially told God, "Not Your will be done but mine!" Like Adam, we want to be our own kings. We don't like anyone telling us what to do, not even God.

Two chapters ago, we saw that Jesus came as our substitute. He obeyed God at the very point where Adam rebelled. In this lesson, we see Jesus in the garden of Gethsemane on the night He was betrayed. Again, through great suffering, Jesus chose to obey the Father's word and to submit to His will.

³² Then they came to a place named Gethsemane, and He told His disciples, "Sit here while I pray." ³³ He took Peter, James, and John with Him, and He began to be deeply distressed and horrified. ³⁴ Then He said to them, "My soul is swallowed up in sorrow—to the point of death. Remain here and stay awake." ³⁵ Then He went a little farther, fell to the ground, and began to pray that if it were possible, the hour might pass from Him. ³⁶ And He said, "Abba, Father! All things are possible for You. Take this cup away from Me. Nevertheless, not what I will, but what You will."

Jesus knew obeying the Father would bring great suffering. That's why He became so deeply distressed and horrified that He told His disciples that He was filled with "sorrow—to the point of death." His agony was rooted in the knowledge that the time was near to fulfill the *purpose* of His death. Jesus did not come in the flesh merely to die; He came to die on behalf of sinners.

The Bible teaches that those who continue in rebellion to God's Word and refuse to submit to God's will are storing up wrath for themselves. One way the Bible describes the outpouring of God's wrath is with the imagery of a cup filled with wine. The wine represents God's wrath/anger (Jer. 25:15-17,28; 49:12). On the day of judgment, God will pour out the cup filled with the wine of His wrath, and He will make rebellious sinners drink every last drop until they become drunk with His wrath (Ps. 75:8; Ezek. 23:32-34).

At the cross (the "hour" that Jesus spoke of), God the Father poured out the full cup of His wrath, which we deserved, on His own Son as a judgment against sin. Anticipating this judgment, Jesus asked His Father, the only One with the authority to remove Him from both *this hour* and *this cup*, if there was any possible way that He could alter His will so that His Word could be fulfilled through some other means.

In the end, however, unlike Adam, Jesus submitted to the Father's will with an emphatic "Not what I will, but what You will." Jesus knew that there was no way to fulfill the Father's Word other than to submit to the Father's will. God could only take this cup away from His people by pouring it out on His righteous Servant (Isa. 51:17,21-22). Jesus received the wounds we deserved, and by faith we receive forgiveness (53:1-12).

Only when we meditate on Christ's life and death (what He has done) are we able to imitate Christ. If we fail to ground our efforts to be like Christ in the good news of what Christ has done for us, we will throw up our hands and give up! The cross is what makes possible our obedience. And the cross shapes what our obedience looks like.

This means that we, like Jesus, are to submit to the Father's will, even when it results in suffering. Because we are called to follow Christ, we are called to suffer (1 Pet. 2:21). Don't be surprised when suffering comes your way! This is one way God slowly transforms us into the image of His Son. The good news is that by His death and resurrection, Jesus has granted us the power to face suffering (vv. 24-25).

▶ IT CAUSED GREAT SHAME (PHIL. 2:5-11).

5 Make your own attitude that of Christ Jesus, 6 who, existing in the form of God, did not consider equality with God as something to be used for His own advantage. 7 Instead He emptied Himself by assuming the form of a slave, taking on the likeness of men. And when He had come as a man in His external form, 8 He humbled Himself by becoming obedient to the point of death—even to death on a cross.

Jesus had all the privileges that came with being God. Yet in submitting to the Father's will, He willingly set those privileges aside in order to become human for our salvation. Jesus did not empty Himself of deity; He took on a lowly status and position as He took on humanity. Jesus had to step out of the glories of heaven, become a servant, and take on flesh. According to the Father's plan of redemption, Jesus had to become like us in order to rescue us.

It may be helpful to think of Jesus' humiliation (incarnation) in this context. Imagine a righteous king who creates a special place, a sanctuary, where he and his people can share together in joy, peace, and love. There is no shame in this sanctuary because there is no evil present; there is only fellowship and joy and life. However, the people are not satisfied with serving the righteous king. They want to be their own kings, so they rebel and seek to establish their own kingdoms.

As punishment for rejecting his rule, the king casts the rebels out of the sanctuary and into a dark kingdom ruled by an evil prince wielding the power of death. Without realizing it, they have become slaves of their own rebellion and of the evil prince who uses the fear of death as a weapon against them.

Because the king loves his people, he chooses to rescue them. But since he is a righteous king, he cannot simply overlook their rebellion. Therefore, in order to rescue the rebels, the king must send his righteous son, the heir to the throne, to this dark realm. In submitting to his father, the righteous son must step away from all his royal privileges. *But he is still the prince; the royal blood flows through his veins.* So in obedience to his father, he enters a different and dark realm where no one acknowledges his authority.

The righteous prince becomes like the captive rebels in order to take their place and rescue them. He obeys all the laws the rebels broke, but he also receives the punishment the rebels deserve. Ultimately the righteous prince must suffer the shame and ridicule of a public trial where the charges against the rebels are read. Then he must face the humiliating, public execution that their crimes require. Only through the son's obedience can the righteous king and the rebels be reconciled.

The Gospel accounts reveal that Jesus is *the* righteous Prince sent by *the* righteous King to rescue a rebellious people held captive by the Evil One. In Philippians 2:5-8, the apostle Paul reminds us that Jesus submitted to the Father's will in humbling Himself in order to rescue us, even though it brought Him great shame. Thankfully our story does not end with Christ's shameful death, for humiliation leads to exaltation.

⁹ For this reason God highly exalted Him and gave Him the name that is above every name, ¹⁰ so that at the name of Jesus every knee should bow—of those who are in heaven and on earth and under the earth— ¹¹ and every tongue should confess that Jesus Christ is Lord, to the glory of God the Father.

God, the righteous King, raised Jesus from the dead, defeating the evil prince, conquering death, and nullifying the fear of death. In fact, because of Jesus' obedient humiliation, the Father exalted Him to the place of ultimate authority. Jesus was crowned Lord and King over all, and the entire universe will bow down to Him and confess His lordship. He who humbled Himself as a servant became the exalted One through His perfect response to God's Word.

▶ IT LEAD TO HIS EXALTATION (HEB. 1:1-4).

It is fascinating to think how often the theme of exaltation through humiliation in the life of Christ is imitated in art. Living with five daughters, I am all too familiar with the story of Cinderella—the daughter who became a servant, who then became a princess. As a man in a house full of girls, I prefer to watch movies like *Gladiator*, which is about a general who became a slave, who became a gladiator, who became the savior of Rome.

Most recently, my older girls and I went to see the movie *Thor*. (My apologies to comic book purists reading this lesson, but I am going to follow the theatrical story line!) Like other fictional stories, *Thor* follows the theme of exaltation through humiliation. Thor is the "god" of thunder, whose father is Odin, the wise, righteous king of the planet Asgard—a place resembling a celestial city. Though Thor is destined to be crowned king of Asgard, his arrogance leads Odin to banish him to earth, where he is stripped of his powers and forced to learn humility. Once the lesson is learned, Thor's god-like powers are returned to him, and he is able to become the hero/savior he was meant to be and return to Asgard to his rightful place next to his father.

All of these stories that people love to tell, generation after generation, are powerful precisely because they follow many of the themes of the true story about our world. The story of God, *the* righteous King, and His Son, Jesus, is the *true* story of exaltation through humiliation. All other stories fall short. They pale in comparison to the story of Jesus.

Notice how the author of Hebrews sets up the story of Jesus.

¹ Long ago God spoke to the fathers by the prophets at different times and in different ways. ² In these last days, He has spoken to us by His Son. God has appointed Him heir of all things and made the universe through Him. ³ The Son is the radiance of God's glory and the exact expression of His nature, sustaining all things by His powerful word. After making purification for sins, He sat down at the right hand of the Majesty on high. ⁴ So He became higher in rank than the angels, just as the name He inherited is superior to theirs.

In order that the world would know Him in all His glory, God has spoken His story to His people throughout history. In the Old Testament era, God spoke through different persons in various, fragmentary ways—fire, smoke, direct word, prophecy, dreams, visions, angels, etc. (Heb. 1:1).

"In these last days" indicates that by His coming, Jesus ushered in the new era of fulfillment that the Old Testament pointed to. In this new era, God has finally and uniquely spoken to us in Jesus Christ, who, as "the radiance of God's glory," is the very presence of God. To know Jesus is to know God; to see Jesus is to see God.

As "the exact expression of His nature," Jesus glorified the Father by revealing the very character of God. It is true that Jesus glorified the Father through His life and ministry. Yet Jesus ultimately and uniquely revealed the character of God in His death and resurrection.

In His death and resurrection, Jesus revealed the Father's justice against human sinfulness and rebellion. At the cross, the Father's righteousness is revealed as He judged sin in Christ; God is both just and the justifier of sinners. Christ's death revealed that God takes sin seriously, and so must we. Forgiveness may be free, but it is not cheap.

In His death and resurrection, Jesus revealed the Father's power and authority over Satan. He came to crush Satan and to set us free from his power. The cross, which at first appears to be Satan's victory, is actually his downfall.

In His death and resurrection, Jesus also revealed the Father's grace and mercy toward undeserving sinners of every ethnicity. By "lifting up" Jesus on the cross, the Father is drawing a multiethnic people to the Son, a people who will be His witnesses to salvation. Now we are commissioned as ambassadors, spreading the good news of His reign to those still in darkness.

Jesus' willing submission to a harsh and shameful death on a cross began His kingly procession to His throne. Once Jesus made purification for sins by receiving the penalty for sin in Himself, His high priestly work was finished, as indicated by the fact that *He sat down*. Having accomplished His atoning work, Jesus sat down *at the right hand* of God—the place of honor.

Jesus, the One who humbled Himself by submitting to the Father, is now the exalted One. As the obedient Son, Jesus has inherited everything in the universe, which was made through Him. As the exalted One who is crowned King of kings and Lord of lords (Phil. 2:9-11), Jesus is superior to the angels (Heb. 1:4,5,14; 2:2-3,18), to Moses (3:1-6; 11:23-29,39), to Joshua (3:7–4:10), to Aaron (5:4), to Melchizedek (chap. 7), to the priests (chaps. 8–9), to the sacrifices (10:1-18), and yes, even Thor. All glory and honor be to King Jesus!

► CONCLUSION

Reverend Henry Maxwell, pastor of the fictional First Church of Raymond, was right. We are called to imitate Christ (1 Pet. 2:21). But if we are to imitate Christ, instead of asking, *"What would Jesus do?"* we should be asking, *"What has Jesus done?"* By focusing on what Jesus has done, we will be able to see the bigger picture of God's plan to glorify Himself through both the humiliation and exaltation of Jesus Christ.

Asking what Jesus has done also moves us to ask, *"Why? Why did Jesus humble Himself, becoming obedient, even unto a harsh and shameful death?"* We have seen the answer to this question in today's lesson. By submitting to the Father's will, Jesus revealed the Father's heart of love for His fallen creation. Though we are the rebels in God's story, God has spoken to us of His love, mercy, and grace in Jesus' death. To be sure, God has also spoken to us about His justice and righteousness in Jesus' death as well.

When we realize that God has spoken to us in Jesus Christ, the natural question is *"What will be our response?"* The appropriate response, of course, is repentance (turning away from our rebellion and our desire to be our own kings) and faith (turning to Christ, bowing down and acknowledging Him as our King). The good news is that those who trust in Christ are exalted with Christ. However, those who reject Christ's rule will receive the full cup of God's wrath (Col. 3:5-7). So then, the question every person must grapple with is not *"What would Jesus do?"* but rather *"What will you do with Jesus?"*

QUESTIONS

1. What would it mean to literally follow "in Christ's steps"? What will imitating Christ cost us? Why is it so important to understand what Jesus would do AND what Jesus has done?

2. Think about the heroes of many American movies and television shows. Many times, the heroes are those who rebel against authority in pursuit of a greater good. How do these stories affect our view of authority? What does submission to God look like in the context of our relationships (dating, parent, teacher, etc.)?

3. Have you ever had to submit to the Father's will knowing it would bring about suffering? How does understanding the purposes of God allow you to face suffering?

4. How does meditating on Christ help you prepare to face suffering now? What does a Christlike response to suffering look like? Are you willing to submit to God's will no matter the cost?

5. Read Hebrews 2:14-18. Why did Jesus have to become like us in order to save us?
6. How does having the attitude of Christ (Phil. 2:5) lead to imitating Christ (vv. 3-4)? Why is it important that we ground our efforts to imitate Christ in the "mind" or "attitude" of Christ?

7. Are you willing to sacrifice personal comfort in order that others might hear of Christ? Are you willing to face humiliation or shame as you follow Christ?

8. In what ways did God speak to His people before Jesus' first coming? In what ways was this revelation only partial?

9. What do you think is the significance of Jesus sitting "down at the right hand of the Majesty on high" in Hebrews 1:3? How does Christ's purification of our sin empower us to submit to God's Word?

10. What should be our response to God's final revelation in Christ? Knowing that Christ has been exalted, what should be our posture toward Him?

Jesus is uniquely able to be our righteousness, succeed where we failed, and restore creation.

Jesus fulfills the law by rightly interpreting it, revealing the true intent, and meeting God's expectations.

When Christ submitted to the Father's Will, it brought great suffering, caused great shame, but lead to His exaltation.

PART 4

OUR REDEEMED RESPONSE TO GOD'S WORD

By God's grace through faith, Christ's perfect response enables us to respond rightly to God's Word. No longer do we consider "What must I do?"; now we say, "Look at what Christ has done." He obeyed God's Word, and now we have a heart to obey out of love and gratitude. We've been redeemed, lifted up, saved in Jesus. Like Him, we now trust, listen to, and submit to God's Word, commune with those who do the same, and proclaim it boldly.

Voices from Church History

"We need to repent of the haughty way in which we sometimes stand in judgment upon Scripture and must learn to sit humbly under its judgment instead. If we come to Scripture with our minds made up, expecting to hear from it only an echo of our own thoughts and never the thunderclap of God's, then indeed he will not speak to us and we shall only be confirmed in our own prejudices. We must allow the Word of God to confront us, to disturb our security, to undermine our complacency and to overthrow our patterns of thought and behavior." [1]

–John Stott (1921-2011)

CHAPTER 10
TRUSTING
Trusting the God Who Speaks

YOU HAVE TO KNOW IT

Acts 7: 2-5 *"Brothers and fathers," he said, "listen: The God of glory appeared to our father Abraham when he was in Mesopotamia, before he settled in Haran, and said to him: Get out of your country and away from your relatives, and come to the land that I will show you. "Then he came out of the land of the Chaldeans and settled in Haran. From there, after his father died, God had him move to this land you now live in. He didn't give him an inheritance in it, not even a foot of ground, but He promised to give it to him as a possession, and to his descendants after him, even though he was childless.*
Finish the story by reading 6-16 in your Bible.

HAVE YOU EVER RECEIVED A gift and had no clue what it was? A few years ago some of my cousins gave my grandmother a Nintendo DS and the game Brain Age for Christmas. When she opened the package, she had no idea what she had been given.

After letting her sit there with a confused look trying to figure that contraption out for a bit, my cousins finally explained the gift. They let her know that it was a portable video game system, and that the game Brain Age was designed to help stimulate brain activity. Since the potential of losing her mental sharpness is one of my grandmother's greatest fears about getting older, the game was a great gift. After she figured out what it was, she was greatly appreciative and has used it regularly.

Notice that last part. She could only truly appreciate and use the gift after she figured out what it was. The same thing is true with the Bible. If we do not know it, we cannot appreciate it, apply it, trust it, or proclaim it.

Look back at our passage. Stephen knew the Bible. In this brief passage, he quickly traces the history of the Christian patriarchs Abraham, Isaac, and Jacob. In the midst of the discussion, he even stops to quote Old Testament passages. The implication is clear: Stephen knew the Word of God!

What about you? Do you know the message and stories that are contained in the Bible? Or is it one of those things that just takes up space on your shelf? In the next few days we'll look at the importance of trusting and proclaiming God's Word. But here's the kicker. If you don't know the Word of God, it's going to be impossible to truly trust and proclaim it.

PAUSE AND REFLECT

▷ **How often do you read God's Word?**

▷ **What can you do to ensure you spend time in God's Word on a regular basis?**

▷ **Will you commit to reading your Bible daily? Why or why not?**

TRUSTING IS DIFFERENT THAN KNOWING

Acts 7:44-51 *"Our ancestors had the tabernacle of the testimony in the wilderness, just as He who spoke to Moses commanded him to make it according to the pattern he had seen. Our ancestors in turn received it and with Joshua brought it in when they dispossessed the nations that God drove out before our fathers, until the days of David. He found favor in God's sight and asked that he might provide a dwelling place for the God of Jacob. But it was Solomon who built Him a house. However, the Most High does not dwell in sanctuaries made with hands, as the prophet says: Heaven is My throne, and earth My footstool. What sort of house will you build for Me? says the Lord, or what is My resting place? Did not My hand make all these things? You stiff-necked people with uncircumcised hearts and ears! You are always resisting the Holy Spirit; as your ancestors did, so do you."*

IF YOU KNOW MUCH ABOUT football, you probably know about "quick slants." For the uninitiated, a "quick slant" is a passing play where a wide receiver runs straight ahead for about two yards, then sharply darts to the inside of the field at a 45 degree angle. The quarterback usually takes three steps backward, and immediately hurls the ball to the receiver just as he is beginning to make the 45 degree turn.

It is a very fast passing play that occurs just seconds after the ball is snapped. In fact, it all occurs so fast that the quarterback has to throw the ball before the receiver ever turns to look at the ball. The quarterback has to fully trust that the receiver is going to run exactly two yards and cut inside at exactly a 45 degree angle. If the receiver is off even slightly, then the ball will fall incomplete, or, even worse, be intercepted.

So why is this important? It demonstrates the difference between knowing something and trusting in something. It is one thing for both the receiver and quarterback to know the play. It is another thing for the quarterback to trust the receiver is going to be where he is supposed to be.

Notice here in our passage how Stephen continues his sermon. As he moves from Bible story to Bible story, mentioning various characters and events, he acknowledges these as real, factual, historical events and people. He doesn't merely know the stories of the Bible, he fully trusts the truthfulness of the stories. He places complete faith in the accuracy of all the events and lives his life in accordance with that faith. This demonstrates a complete trust of God's Word!

PAUSE AND REFLECT

▷ What is the difference between knowing Bible facts and trusting the truth of the Bible?

▷ Why is it important to trust that the Bible is true?

▷ Does your life show that you trust the truth of the Bible? How can we learn to trust the Bible and apply it to our lives?

SPEAK WITH BOLDNESS

Acts 7:52-56 *"Which of the prophets did your fathers not persecute? They even killed those who announced beforehand the coming of the Righteous One, whose betrayers and murderers you have now become. You received the law under the direction of angels and yet have not kept it." When they heard these things, they were enraged in their hearts and gnashed their teeth at him. But Stephen, filled by the Holy Spirit, gazed into heaven. He saw God's glory, with Jesus standing at the right hand of God, and he said, "Look! I see the heavens opened and the Son of Man standing at the right hand of God!"*
Finish the story by reading 57-60 in your Bible.

IMAGINE YOU'VE BEEN ASKED TO serve as the campaign manager for an upcoming election. Think for a moment about what that would entail.

First, you would have to know the person and some info about them. It may be common sense, but it would be impossible to be the campaign manager for a person that you don't know.

Second, you would have to trust the person. As campaign manager, if you are going to devote your time and energy into getting this person elected, you have to be able to trust the candidate. You have to trust that they are genuinely going to try to solve the issues that they are campaigning on. By agreeing to be the campaign manager, you are putting your name on the line as well, trusting that the candidate will not ruin your name.

Finally, you have to proclaim the worthiness of the candidate. This is, after all, your real job. The entire purpose of the campaign manager is to tell the world about why your candidate would be best. You ultimate goal is to figure out the best way possible to proclaim the worthiness of your candidate.

Did you notice that in order to do the ultimate job of campaigning for the candidate, you first had to know the person and trust the person? We find this exact same process when dealing with God's word. We cannot proclaim the Word of God without knowing and trusting it. Stephen demonstrated this perfectly. His ultimate goal was to boldly proclaim the gospel of Christ. He was able to make this proclamation because he knew and trusted the Bible. God desires each and every one of us to boldly proclaim the gospel. If we are to be obedient in this endeavor, we must be committed to this mantra: Know - Trust - Proclaim.

PAUSE AND REFLECT

▷ Why is it important to proclaim God's word?

▷ Why do we have to know and trust God's word before we proclaim it?

▷ What are you doing to proclaim God's word on a regular basis? What keeps you from speaking about God?

TRUSTING THE GOD WHO SPEAKS

We demonstrate our trust in God's Word when we know it, when we believe it, and when we proclaim it boldly.

GROUND-LEVEL—that's where life begins. Wide-eyed and full of awe, we spend 12 months crawling on hands and knees.

Eventually we learn to stand, to balance, to walk and jog and run. From elliptical machines and ice skates to tennis shoes and roller blades, sooner or later, our abilities increase. However, the taller we grow and the faster we go, the less we return to our knees. In the end, we as adults exchange a world of ground-level for a world of eye-level, and we often forget the beauty of humility.

Stephen knew something about "ground-level." As the first Christian martyr, Stephen proclaimed with great boldness the faith that eventually cost his life. Although his name means "crown," Stephen understood that Christ's followers cannot wear the crown without carrying the cross. For him, like all Christians, *the way up is the way down.*

Jesus once said, "If anyone wants to come with Me, he must deny himself, take up his cross, and follow Me" (Matt. 16:24). Following in the footsteps of his Savior, Stephen knew that faithfulness before God is more important than popularity before men. He knew that the proper posture toward God's Holy Word is repentance for sin and trust in Jesus Christ. Stephen returned to his knees—physically and spiritually. And then God worked powerfully through Stephen's life and witness.

Stephen's testimony offers us a 3-D Christianity. He shows us that following Jesus Christ involves three dimensions: information, transformation, and proclamation. Stephen believed the good news about Christ (information), loved Christ (transformation), and preached Christ (proclamation). Likewise, we have the opportunity to give our heads, hearts, and lips to the God who creates us and re-creates us.

In this chapter, we'll explore Stephen's three-dimensional Christianity as he demonstrates his knowledge of God's Word, his trust in its transformational truth, and his passion to preach the gospel not only with his lips but also with his life. The goal of this chapter is to show how God's Word affects every aspect of who we are.

We demonstrate our trust in God's word...

▶ **WHEN WE KNOW IT (ACTS 7:2-16).**

Let's begin by looking at Stephen's sermon in Acts 7:2-16. As you read Acts 7:2-16, ask the group to notice the biblical details that Stephen knew by heart. Highlight the importance of understanding the grand narrative of Scripture.

² "Brothers and fathers," he said, "listen: The God of glory appeared to our father Abraham when he was in Mesopotamia, before he settled in Haran, ³and said to him: Get out of your country and away from your relatives, and come to the land that I will show you.

⁴ "Then he came out of the land of the Chaldeans and settled in Haran. From there, after his father died, God had him move to this land you now live in. ⁵He didn't give him an inheritance in it, not even a foot of ground, but He promised to give it to him as a possession, and to his descendants after him, even though he was childless. ⁶God spoke in this way: His descendants would be strangers in a foreign country, and they would enslave and oppress them for ⁴⁰⁰ years. ⁷I will judge the nation that they will serve as slaves, God said. After this, they will come out and worship Me in this place. ⁸Then He gave him the covenant of circumcision. After this, he fathered Isaac and circumcised him on the eighth day; Isaac did the same with Jacob, and Jacob with the ¹² patriarchs.

⁹ "The patriarchs became jealous of Joseph and sold him into Egypt, but God was with him ¹⁰and rescued him out of all his troubles. He gave him favor and wisdom in the sight of Pharaoh, king of Egypt, who appointed him ruler over Egypt and over his whole household. ¹¹Then a famine and great suffering came over all of Egypt and Canaan, and our ancestors could find no food. ¹²When Jacob heard there was grain in Egypt, he sent our ancestors the first time. ¹³The second time, Joseph was revealed to his brothers, and Joseph's family became known to Pharaoh. ¹⁴Joseph then invited his father Jacob and all his relatives, ⁷⁵ people in all, ¹⁵and Jacob went down to Egypt. He and our ancestors died there, ¹⁶were carried back to Shechem, and were placed in the tomb that Abraham had bought for a sum of silver from the sons of Hamor in Shechem.

Bible memory is vitally important for believers, and it's not merely because we need to know a few isolated verses. Easy recall of the grand narrative of Scripture is life-transforming. Knowing the big picture of the story the Bible tells is what transforms our worldview so that we are able to look at the world through Bible-shaped eyes.

Notice how easily Stephen recalled the details of his people's history. He stood on the promises God had made to Abraham. He recognized the nature of the covenant. He even knew the number of people in Joseph's family who migrated to Egypt (75 to be exact!). Stephen knew the Bible as a whole and in its parts, and that's why his sermon was so powerful.

The Bible is powerful, which is why the apostle Paul likened it to a sword. Jesus turned to the Word when He was tempted in the wilderness. In His moment of trial, when Christ felt the fatigue full force, the Scripture proved energizing. In His moment of hunger, the Word of God proved satisfying and sharp—razor blade sharp. It was sharp enough to fend off temptations, ward off demons, and even cut the Evil One himself.

There were no "amens" or "hallelujahs" or calls of "preach it, brother" at the end of Stephen's sermon. In fact, instead of listening for long, his audience reached for weapons to kill him. Beginning with Abraham, Isaac, and Jacob, Stephen presented a panorama of the Old Testament. He explained the history of the Israelites, Joseph's slavery in Egypt, and the Israelites' exodus to the promised land. Stephen knew his Bible backwards and forwards. And his sermon teaches an important truth about God's Word. When difficulty comes, the testimonies of Scripture encourage and remind God's people of God's faithfulness.

J. I. Packer once said that Christianity in America is "three thousand miles wide and one inch deep." Can the same be said about your knowledge of Scripture? Most of us know the "mountain peak passages" that rise above the landscape of Scripture. But hidden in the valleys of Scripture—in the canyons of the canon—are equally powerful truths. So we must go deeper. We must explore the entirety of God's Word because His glory is everywhere, and it brings life to our souls.

In difficult times, Gods' Words can provide great comfort. Without a knowledge of His Word, that same comfort is going to be difficult to find. Challenge the students to commit a passage of scripture to memory. Next time you meet, ask for volunteers to share what they memorized, and begin with what you committed to memory.

▶ WHEN WE BELIEVE IT (ACTS 7:44-51).

44 "Our ancestors had the tabernacle of the testimony in the wilderness, just as He who spoke to Moses commanded him to make it according to the pattern he had seen. 45 Our ancestors in turn received it and with Joshua brought it in when they dispossessed the nations that God drove out before our fathers, until the days of David. 46 He found favor in God's sight and asked that he might provide a dwelling place for the God of Jacob. 47 But it was Solomon who built Him a house. 48 However, the Most High does not dwell in sanctuaries made with hands, as the prophet says: [49] *Heaven is My throne, and earth My footstool. What sort of house will you build for Me? says the Lord, or what is My resting place?* [50] *Did not My hand make all these things?*

[51] *"You stiff-necked people with uncircumcised hearts and ears! You are always resisting the Holy Spirit; as your ancestors did, so do you.*

Have you ever leaned against the wind? I mean *really* leaned? Having lived in St. Andrews, Scotland, for three years, I can tell you from experience that it's possible. Once on a gusty day, I stood on the beach where the wind was most forceful. The water churned against the beach, struggling beneath the violent gale. With arms outstretched, I turned my back to the North Sea and gave my weight to gravity. To my amazement, I discovered that the wind—so invisible and untouchable—leaned right back against me and sustained my diagonal posture.

Jesus once compared the Holy Spirit to the wind that "blows where it pleases" (John 3:8). It was this same Spirit that hovered over the surface of the waters (Gen. 1:2), that breathed life into Adam's lungs, and that inspired the writers of the Bible—"Men spoke from God," wrote Peter, "as they were moved by the Holy Spirit" (2 Pet. 1:21).

Theologians call this concept "inspiration." It's the idea that God divinely inspired His Word. Make no mistake about it, God is the ultimate Author of His Book. But God enlisted a variety of writers to pen His words.

In Stephen's sermon, we see that he took for granted the origin of the Bible. He knew sure enough that it came from God through men. Yet he also took for granted the veracity of the biblical account. Notice in this passage how he clearly assumes the factual nature of the Bible's story line. Moving from Moses to Joshua to Solomon, Stephen's sermon builds upon the solid foundation of biblical teaching and climaxes with a clear diagnosis of his listeners' resistance to the Holy Spirit.

As Christians, we submit to the Holy Spirit as He speaks to us through His Word. Everything that God tells us in the Bible is true. We call this **the doctrine of inerrancy**. Paul tells us in 2 Timothy 3:16 that the Bible is "God-breathed." What does this mean? It means that God's Word originates from God's breath. Those who deny inerrancy are saying, in effect, that God has breathed out something false, something impure. Instead, God's breath is pure, holy, flawless, and true. If God breathes something into existence, whether it's a word or a world, in its original form it's going to come out perfect.

Because God's Word is inspired, inerrant, and authoritative, you and I can lean hard against it. We can trust the truth we read in the Bible. Like Stephen we can believe that what the Bible says happened really happened.

► WHEN WE PROCLAIM IT BOLDLY (ACTS 7:52-60).

⁵² Which of the prophets did your fathers not persecute? They even killed those who announced beforehand the coming of the Righteous One, whose betrayers and murderers you have now become. ⁵³ You received the law under the direction of angels and yet have not kept it."

⁵⁴ When they heard these things, they were enraged in their hearts and gnashed their teeth at him. ⁵⁵ But Stephen, filled by the Holy Spirit, gazed into heaven. He saw God's glory, with Jesus standing at the right hand of God, and he said, ⁵⁶ "Look! I see the heavens opened and the Son of Man standing at the right hand of God!"

⁵⁷ Then they screamed at the top of their voices, covered their ears, and together rushed against him. ⁵⁸ They threw him out of the city and began to stone him. And the witnesses laid their robes at the feet of a young man named Saul. ⁵⁹ They were stoning Stephen as he called out: "Lord Jesus, receive my spirit!" ⁶⁰ Then he knelt down and cried out with a loud voice, "Lord, do not charge them with this sin!" And saying this, he fell asleep.

We live in a Scripture-saturated society. We've got dozens of translations and dozens of covers: brown leather, alligator leather, olive wood, Velcro, duct tape. We produce Bibles for preschoolers, college students, young adults, apologists, archeologists, athletes. We buy one-year Bibles, interlinear Bibles, amplified, simplified, limited edition Bibles. Christians have so many Bible options that we take them for granted; we often devalue them and neglect to read them.

Stephen shows us that knowing God with our heads is not enough. Even the demons know there is one God (Jas. 2:19). Rather, Stephen teaches us that knowledge of God never remains in the abstract. Knowledge must become trust. Trust must become love. And just as when you love someone, you cannot help but talk about Him. You cannot help but talk *to* Him. And that is the place where God's pursuit of us becomes our witness for Him, a place where transformation leads to proclamation.

Some have mistakenly attributed a saying to the twelfth-century preacher and friar Francis of Assisi; it qualified Jesus' Great Commission this way: "Preach the gospel always, and if necessary use words." Although this statement might have originally been directed to preachers who only spoke about God but did not live out their faith, it is important for us to realize that *words are at the core of the Christian faith.* The words of God (Scripture) reveal the Word of God (Christ). Stephen shows us that humility and submission to God's Word are crucial for every believer and that humility and submission are transformed into bold proclamation of the truth.

▶ CONCLUSION

In the early sixteenth century, German artist Matthias Grünewald painted the "Isenheim Altarpiece." If you look on the right of the painting, you will see the figure of an austere monk—John the Baptist. In his left hand, he's holding the Scriptures. At the end of his outstretched arm is an outstretched finger, and at the end of his outstretched finger is an outstretched Savior hanging on a cross. And in the background are the words "He must increase. I must decrease."

Stephen also held tightly to God's Word while pointing to Christ. He is an example of a repentant believer who returned to his knees, who bowed down in humility before God. Like Stephen, you and I have the privilege of doing the same thing. We have the opportunity of living life in 3-D: knowing God with our heads, loving God with our hearts, and sharing God with our lips. And as we radically abandon ourselves to God's mission, as we keep pointing to Christ with our lives, we can be confident that through our trust in God's Word, the Holy Spirit will use the Holy Scripture to make us whole and holy.

QUESTIONS

1. Which of these dimensions (believing in Christ, loving Christ, preaching Christ) do you find easiest? Which do you find most difficult? Why?

2. In Paul's list of spiritual armor (Eph. 6:10-17), why is Scripture compared to a sword? Reflect on Hebrews 4:12. In what ways does Scripture divide "soul and spirit, joints and marrow"?

3. Do you set aside time to spend with Scripture? Do you set aside space where you open your Bible and listen to God from His Word?

4. It follows that the better we know the Bible, the better we know the God of the Bible. In what ways can our knowledge of Scripture influence the way we worship God, both privately and corporately? How can we best demonstrate the we believe the Bible to be true? In what ways might your actions be displaying that you don't believe the Bible to be true?

5. How can we make sure that the Scriptures that come into our hands also come out of our mouths?

6. How essential to following Christ is "sharing the gospel"? Why is the vocalizing of faith so vital for citizens of God's kingdom?

7. Respond to the following statement: "Preaching the gospel without words is like sending a text message without letters."

8. Which of the these areas is most difficult for you: knowing God with your head, loving God with your heart or sharing God with your lips?

9. What can you do to grow in that area?

10. How can you better demonstrate you trust God's word?

CHAPTER 11

SUBMITTING
Submitting to the God Who Speaks

BETTER THAN GOOGLE

Heb. 4:12 *"For the word of God is living and effective and sharper than any double-edged sword, penetrating as far as the separation of soul and spirit, joints and marrow. It is able to judge the ideas and thoughts of the heart."*
Also read 2 Kings 22:3-10 in your Bible.

DO YOU KNOW WHERE GOOGLE Got Its Name? The name Google is derived from the number "googol". A googol is the number one followed by 100 zeros, or, in scientific notation, 1×10^{100}. When the founders of Google were looking for a name, they decided upon Google to convey the message that they were searching an extraordinary number of webpages every time someone used their search engine.

So how big is a googol, exactly? Well, for some perspective, the number of electrons in the entire known universe is estimated to be around 1×10^{79}. Remember, electrons are one of the components of atoms. That means every single atom has at least one electron, and most have many electrons. If you were to add those up for the entire universe, the number would be 1×10^{79}. Significantly less than a googol.

Why is this important? It will help us to see how incredible the Word of God is. Throughout the Old Testament, approximately 300 different prophecies regarding the Messiah are presented. In the New Testament, we find that Jesus fulfilled every single one of these prophecies. The mathematical odds of all of these prophecies being fulfilled are literally incalculable.

So we ask again, why does this matter? Well, the Bible is the only collection of writings ever to exist that forecast the future with such clarity and precision. Think about it for a moment. The Bible is a single work that was written over a span of 1500 years, by more than 40 different authors, in a variety of locales, in different cultural settings, in many different moods, across three different continents, in three different languages, in a variety of literary styles, and in response to a multitude of controversial subjects. Yet, in spite of this, it tells one central story of God's redemption of man without a single error or contradiction.

In other words, when we pick up our Bibles, we can be completely confident that we are reading the true Word of God!

PAUSE AND REFLECT

▷ Why is is important that the Bible tells the truth?

▷ How does the truthfulness of the Bible impact your daily life?

SHARPER THAN A GINSU

2 Kings 22:11-13 *"When the king heard the words of the book of the law, he tore his clothes. Then he commanded Hilkiah the priest, Ahikam son of Shaphan, Achbor son of Micaiah, Shaphan the court secretary, and the king's servant Asaiah: 'Go and inquire of the Lord for me, the people, and all Judah about the instruction in this book that has been found. For great is the Lord's wrath that is kindled against us because our ancestors have not obeyed the words of this book in order to do everything written about us.' "*

HAVE YOU HEARD OF THE Ginsu Knife? A quick search of Youtube will provide the original commercials of these knives. The maker of these knives claimed they could cut through just about anything without dulling their blades.

On the commercials, you'll see these knives cut through all kinds of things, including frozen vegetables, tree branches, nails, leather shoes, the bones in T-bone steaks, soda cans, and even the head of a hammer. It takes a pretty incredible (and sharp) knife to slice through all of these objects!

Notice what Hebrews says about God's Word. It says that its sharper than any two-edged sword. In other words, God's Word cuts deeper than any Ginsu knife could ever cut. It cuts through everything we encounter in this world, and penetrates our hearts. God's Word slices through our body and exposes the sinful condition of our hearts.

No matter how deep we try to bury our sins, God's Word cuts through and exposes them. And that is a wonderful thing. By cutting through our entire being and revealing the sins we've committed, we can be confronted by the gospel of Christ. The good news of Christ isn't that He came to save a bunch of good people. The good news is that "while we were still sinners Christ died for us" (Rom. 5:8)!

This demonstrates an important reason for studying the Scriptures. As we learn more and more about who God is, we see the impossibility of becoming like Him on our own. The Bible shows us how desperately we need a Savior!

PAUSE AND REFLECT

▷ What does the Bible reveal about our hearts?

▷ Why is it so important to realize the sinful condition of our hearts?

▷ How has sin affected the world as a whole?

▷ What can we do to overcome the sinful condition of our hearts?

ANTI-VENOM FOR SIN?

Heb. 4:13 *"No creature is hidden from Him, but all things are naked and exposed to the eyes of Him to whom we must give an account."*
Also read 2 Kings 22:14-20 in your Bible.

I HAVE AN INTERESTING RELATIONSHIP with snakes. I am absolutely terrified of them, yet am incredibly fascinated by them all at the same time. In the real world, that means if I encounter a snake, I run in the other direction as fast as humanly possible. But, if I'm protected by plexiglass at the zoo or stumble upon a snake show on Animal Planet, I'm enthralled.

This fascination has led to the watching of many television programs of people getting bitten by venomous snakes. Once bitten, the need for anti-venom quickly becomes apparent. Once the person can get to the hospital and the anti-venom is injected, the person begins down the road to recovery.

Compare this to the human condition. We've all been bitten by the poison of sin. Sin has entered our hearts at birth and colors everything we do. It moves throughout our body and soul, destroying everything in its path. Fortunately, God has provided the ultimate combatant to sin: His only begotten Son. Jesus came to earth, lived a sinless life, died on the cross, and rose again in order to forgive us of our sins. In other words, He is the perfect treatment to all the sin in the world.

But notice a key element in the process of recovering from a snakebite. The existence of anti-venom is not sufficient for recovery. The anti-venom must be injected into the person. In this instance, the syringe is the instrument that enables the anti-venom to enter the bloodstream and begin its healing properties. The syringe itself doesn't heal the person, but it makes it possible for the anti-venom to do its job.

In many ways, this scenario parallels with the Bible. Christ alone is the solution to man's problem of sin. But the Bible is the tool that enables us to see both our sinful condition and point us to the ultimate healer and redeemer, Jesus Christ.

That is the main thrust of the entire Bible. Yes it is entirely true. Yes it points out our sinful condition. Yes it tells us about the world, morality, history, and a multitude of other things. But above everything else, it allows us to encounter the life-changing truth of the gospel.

PAUSE AND REFLECT

▷ **Why is the Bible important?**

▷ **Does owning a Bible do anything for you?**

▷ **How does the Bible communicate the gospel to the world around us?**

SUBMITTING TO THE GOD WHO SPEAKS

When we submit our lives to God we accept His truths, He changes our heart, and He continues to refine us.

DID YOU KNOW that policemen in India are paid higher salaries if they can grow out their mustaches? Why? Because according to Mayank Jain, a police chief in India, mustaches command authority and foster "a positive and masterful impression on the local people."[1]

This may not be your experience with mustaches. Many times mustaches make people look a little creepy. What are your thoughts on guys with mustaches? It is interesting how culturally a mustache doesn't invoke the same feelings for us as it does in India. While mustaches in India give a person an air of authority, what would you say creates that same feel in our culture.

For thousands of years, God's people have been asking the question "By what authority?" By what authority should the Holy Scriptures be judged? By *whose* authority should theology, the gospel, ministry, and missions be judged?

Moses faced this question—"Who made you a leader and judge over us?" (Ex. 2:14). Peter and John faced this question—"By what power or in what name have you done this?" (Acts 4:7). Even Jesus Himself had to answer this question—"Who gave You this authority to do these things?" (Mark 11:28). Every one of God's people must address the question "By what authority?" How will you respond?

WHEN WE SUBMIT OUR LIVES TO GOD...

▶ WE ACCEPT HIS TRUTHS (HEB. 4:12; 2 KINGS 22:3-10).

12 For the word of God is living and effective and sharper than any double-edged sword, penetrating as far as the separation of soul and spirit, joints and marrow. It is able to judge the ideas and thoughts of the heart.

3 In the eighteenth year of King Josiah, the king sent the court secretary Shaphan son of Azaliah, son of Meshullam, to the LORD's temple, saying, 4 "Go up to Hilkiah the high priest so that he may total up the money brought into the LORD's temple—

the money the doorkeepers have collected from the people. ⁵ It is to be put into the hands of those doing the work—those who oversee the LORD's temple. They in turn are to give it to the workmen in the LORD's temple to repair the damage. ⁶ They are to give it to the carpenters, builders, and masons to buy timber and quarried stone to repair the temple. ⁷ But no accounting is to be required from them for the money put into their hands since they work with integrity."

⁸ Hilkiah the high priest told Shaphan the court secretary, "I have found the book of the law in the LORD's temple," and he gave the book to Shaphan, who read it.

⁹ Then Shaphan the court secretary went to the king and reported, "Your servants have emptied out the money that was found in the temple and have put it into the hand of those doing the work—those who oversee the LORD's temple." ¹⁰ Then Shaphan the court secretary told the king, "Hilkiah the priest has given me a book," and Shaphan read it in the presence of the king.

In 1902, a paleontologist named Barnum Brown made a surprising discovery in Hell Creek, Montana. Later named the "world's greatest dinosaur hunter," Brown unearthed the skeleton of a "large Carnivorous Dinosaur." He unearthed a second, fuller specimen in 1908. Unlike other dinosaurs he discovered, this forty-five-foot-long monster (aka *Tyrannosaurus rex*) was a "king of the period and a monarch of its race," boasting a four-foot-long skull with six-inch-long teeth. It was the greatest discovery of his life, a discovery that forever changed the way dinosaurs were studied in the future.[3]

Almost three thousand years earlier, a high priest named Hilkiah also made an important discovery. During the renovation of Solomon's Temple, Hilkiah stumbled upon a scroll that had been hidden for centuries. This was no ordinary manuscript. To Hilkiah's surprise, the scroll happened to be the long-lost Book of the Law, the writings that Moses passed down to Joshua (see Josh. 1:6-8).

We live in a culture of upgrades. Take, for instance, the faithful laptop these words were written on. A MacBook Pro, 2.66 GHz, Intel Core 2 Duo. A fine piece of machinery, for sure. But an outdated one. There's always something faster on the market, something newer. Our culture values upgrading, and whether it's the latest iPhone or the latest fashion, new things seem to have authority over old things.

C. S. Lewis once said that some things in this world are permanent and eternal. He called them "first things."[5] King Josiah understood that God's Word was a first thing, a primary thing that contains truth that transcends time and place. When Josiah heard about the discovery of the scroll, he understood its significance and ordered Shaphan, the secretary of the court, to read it aloud in Josiah's presence.

Josiah's response to the discovery of the scroll teaches us that the Word of God is our final authority, the standard by which all things are judged—even us. The Bible *is* old, but the Bible never *gets* old. You and I can examine and scrutinize the Scriptures, but God's Word also examines and scrutinizes us. Since God is the author of His Word, to disobey or disbelieve Scripture is to disobey and disbelieve God.

▶ THE AUTHORITY OF SCRIPTURE

Think about the word *authority*. Do you see another word inside it? *Author.* The Bible has authority because God is the Author. It's true that God spoke through human authors in order to get His message across. But ultimately it is *God's* message revealed in the Scriptures. The Bible has authority because God is the Author, the Creator, the ultimate source of all authority.

Pastor Joshua Harris writes: "The doctrine of Scripture teaches us about the authority of God's Word. Scripture must be the final rule of faith and practice for our lives. Not our feelings or emotions. Not signs or prophetic words or hunches. What more can God give us than what he's given in Scripture? The question is, will we listen? Will we obey when we don't like what the Bible has to say? This is a moment when our belief about Scripture meets reality. What we *say* we believe makes very little difference until we act on our belief. I suppose most Christians would say that the Bible is the authoritative Word of God. But until this authority actually changes how we live— how we think and act—talk of the authority of Scripture is nothing but a bunch of religious lingo. We're treating the God-breathed Word of God like a lot of hot air."[6]

When push comes to shove, we show what we really believe about the Bible by how we act. We can say that we believe the Bible is true and authoritative and therefore we are to submit to it, but what we affirm about God's Word can be denied by actions that undercut the Bible's authoritativeness. If the Bible is true and if it is truly authoritative, it must change the way we live.

▶ HE CHANGES OUR HEART (HEB. 4:12; 2 KINGS 22:11-13).

[12] For the word of God is living and effective and sharper than any double-edged sword, penetrating as far as the separation of soul and spirit, joints and marrow. It is able to judge the ideas and thoughts of the heart.

[11] When the king heard the words of the book of the law, he tore his clothes. [12] Then he commanded Hilkiah the priest, Ahikam son of Shaphan, Achbor son of Micaiah, Shaphan the court secretary, and the king's servant Asaiah: [13] "Go and inquire of the LORD for me, the people, and all Judah about the instruction in this book that has been found. For great is the LORD's wrath that is kindled against us because our ancestors have not obeyed the words of this book in order to do everything written about us."

In feudal Japan, it could take up to a whole year for a blacksmith to forge a single samurai sword. Unlike Roman, Viking, or Arabian swords, the *katana* (also called "Japanese steel") was heated and folded thousands of times until most of the impurities were hammered out. That's why the samurai sword could slice through anything in its path.[9]

The author of Hebrews tells us that God's Word is "sharper than any double-edged sword, penetrating as far as the separation of soul and spirit, joints and marrow" (4:12). Although it could take a full year to forge a samurai sword, God spent over 2,000 years forging His Holy Word—a pure and perfect weapon without flaw or impurity.

We call this truth the **infallibility of Scripture.** It's the idea that God's Word is pure in its authority and authoritative in its purity. In other words, God's weapon contains no deficiencies inherent to its design, construction, and effectiveness. It pierces its target every time, for God said, "My word that comes from My mouth will not return to Me empty, but it will accomplish what I please and will prosper in what I send it to do" (Isa. 55:11).

Jesus once said that the "mouth speaks from the overflow of the heart" (Luke 6:45). Because God's Word flows from God's heart, we can be confident that the Bible is the ultimate standard of truth.

The "sword of the Spirit, which is God's word" (Eph. 6:17) is a powerful weapon against Satan (see Matt. 4:1-11), but it is also capable of piercing the hearts of God's people. Look at Acts 2:37. After Peter proclaimed the gospel to the crowd, we read that "they came under deep conviction," and then they repented. The same thing happened to King Josiah after he heard the reading of God's Word. Having realized that his people had provoked God to wrath by not keeping the laws of God, Josiah tore his clothes, a sign of humility and repentance.

The tearing of Josiah's clothes foreshadowed a future event when the Roman soldiers tore up and "divided [Christ's] clothes" (Luke 23:34). Jesus embodied a spirit of humility. We see it not only in His words—"The gentle are blessed, for they will inherit the earth" (Matt. 5:5) and "I am gentle and humble in heart" (11:29)—but also in His actions, for He "humbled Himself by becoming obedient to the point of death—even to death on a cross" (Phil. 2:8).

Both Josiah's and Jesus' clothes were torn on behalf of their people's sins. However, the tearing of Christ's clothes was not out of repentance but rather out of forgiveness: "Father, forgive them," said Jesus, "because they do not know what they are doing" (Luke 23:34).

Amazing love! The selfless trajectory of grace and sacrifice. When Christ absorbed the sins of His people, the temple curtain was torn from top to bottom and sinners were granted access into the presence of God.

Two thousand years later, the Holy Spirit continues to remind us of this event by convicting us of our sins and using God's samurai-sharp Word to penetrate our hearts, judge our thoughts, remove our impurities, and bring us to a place of repentance and ultimate healing in Jesus.

The perfect Word of God shows us our imperfections and gives us a true diagnosis of our fallen state. Whereas the world often tells us that our problem is failing to believe in ourselves, the Bible gives us a stark picture of our true state: we are in rebellion against God. In this way, the Bible cuts to the heart of our sinful condition.

It may be appealing to agree with the world and to think we're not as bad as the Bible says we are, but as Trevin Wax points out, this watered-down understanding of sin actually robs us of the beauty of God's grace: "What looks more glorious? A God who loves us by ignoring our sin? Or a God who pays the enormous debt for our sin by taking it upon Himself? When sin is seen as the rebellion it is, grace is costly—and transformative! When sin is shrunken to the point that our accountability to God is removed, then grace is cheap, and it leaves us unchanged."[11]

We need the Word of God to provide us with the stark reality of our fallen condition. Ignoring the Bible's teaching about sin is like ignoring a serious diagnosis from an expert doctor. But thankfully the Bible doesn't just tell us about our fallen state, it also leads us to the prescription: repentance and faith.

▶ HE CONTINUES TO REFINE US (HEB. 4:13; 2 KINGS 22:14-20)

13 No creature is hidden from Him, but all things are naked and exposed to the eyes of Him to whom we must give an account.

14 So Hilkiah the priest, Ahikam, Achbor, Shaphan, and Asaiah went to the prophetess Huldah, wife of Shallum son of Tikvah, son of Harhas, keeper of the wardrobe. She lived in Jerusalem in the Second District. They spoke with her.

15 She said to them, "This is what the LORD God of Israel says, 'Say to the man who sent you to Me: 16 This is what the LORD says: I am about to bring disaster on this place and on its inhabitants, fulfilling all the words of the book that the king of Judah has read, 17 because they have abandoned Me and burned incense to other gods in order to provoke Me with all the work of their hands. My wrath will be kindled against this place, and it will not be quenched. 18 Say this to the king of Judah who sent you to inquire of the LORD: This is what the LORD God of Israel says: As for the words that you heard, 19 because your heart was tender and you humbled yourself before the LORD when you heard what I spoke against this place and against its inhabitants, that they would become a desolation and a curse, and because you have torn your clothes and wept before Me, I Myself have heard you—this is the LORD's declaration— 20 therefore, I will indeed gather you to your fathers, and you will be gathered to your grave in peace. Your eyes will not see all the disaster that I am bringing on this place.'" Then they reported to the king.

Controversial as they might be, backscatter X-ray detectors have become the latest advance in airport security. Also known as the "whole body imager" (WBI), this machine detects ionized radiation reflected from objects and then creates a three-dimensional image of those objects. In other words, if you're packing heat in an airport, the WBI is going to see it.

The author of Hebrews says, "all things are naked and exposed to the eyes of Him to whom we must give an account" (4:13). All things. That means you—and me! Job said, "For His eyes watch over a man's ways, and He observes all his steps. There is no darkness, no deep darkness, where evildoers can hide themselves" (Job 34:21-22).

God sees through all of us all of the time. Every thought, every action, every hidden sin and secret is known and perfectly perceived by the all-knowing eye of the Almighty. It is a dangerous thing to stand naked in the presence of a powerful God.

Isaiah discovered this to be true when he looked up and "saw the Lord seated on a high and lofty throne, and His robe filled the temple" (Isa. 6:1). What was the first thing out of Isaiah's mouth? "Woe is me for I am ruined because I am a man of unclean lips" (v. 5). In the presence of God, even the angelic seraphim had to shield themselves from God's glorious light.

King Josiah sought light for his people. He knew that unless he humbled himself before the presence of God on behalf of his people, God would destroy them. A day of reckoning was coming. But when God saw Josiah's repentance, He said, "because you have torn your clothes and wept before Me, I Myself have heard you" (2 Kings 22:19).

The joy of salvation is that God does not look at His people without a filter. Instead, the Father sees believers through the lens of Jesus Christ's righteousness. The Messiah's atonement shields us from the wrath of God. Despite our manifold sins and our rebellious natures, God is "patient…not wanting any to perish, but all to come to repentance" (2 Pet. 3:9).

Jesus once said, "Unless you repent, you will all perish" (Luke 13:3,5). The Greek word for "repent" in this passage can be broken into two words: *meta* (a preposition that means "after" or "with") and *noeo* (a verb that means "to think" or "to perceive"). When these two words are combined, the compound word connotes a significant shift of thinking and action, a dynamic "changing of one's mind."

▶ CONCLUSION

Of whom did Jesus say, "I have not found so great a faith even in Israel!" (Luke 7:9)? Was it Peter, James, or John? Perhaps it was Mary or Martha. No. This honor went to a random officer in the Roman army, a centurion. We don't know much about this centurion; in fact, we don't even know his name. But what we do know is that this Roman officer recognized the authority of Jesus better than anyone else Jesus had met, even the disciples.

When the centurion's slave was sick, he sent his friends to tell Jesus, "Lord, don't trouble Yourself, since I am not worthy to have You come under my roof. That is why I didn't even consider myself worthy to come to You. But say the word, and my servant will be cured. For I too am a man placed under authority, having soldiers under my command. I say to this one, 'Go!' and he goes; and to another, 'Come!' and he comes; and to my slave, 'Do this!' and he does it" (vv. 6-8).

Why did Christ pay him the compliment "I have not found so great a faith even in Israel!"? Because this centurion knew the answer to the question "By what authority?" By what authority can my sick slave become well again? Not by Satan's authority. Not by Caesar's authority. Not by tradition's authority. Not even by religion's authority. The supreme authority in heaven and earth belongs to God alone.

Ultimate authority does not come from man-made institutions. It does not come from power, wealth, social status, or reputation. It certainly doesn't come from an ability to grow out a mustache! Instead, all authority under heaven and earth belongs to God, and you and I submit to the God who speaks by reading and obeying the Word He has spoken.

QUESTIONS

1. How does one become "an authority" on a certain subject or topic? How do your parents exercise authority over you? What is the difference between authority that is earned and authority inherent to a position?

2. Would your attitude toward Scripture change if it were extremely difficult to obtain a copy? How so? What if it were illegal to own a copy of the Bible?

3. What piece of technology do you want to get next? How is it better than what you currently have? Describe a time when the newer upgrade wasn't better than the original?

4. What would you say to someone who thinks Scripture is just an outdated book—a dinosaur—that might have been powerful long ago but lacks relevance today?

5. When John was on the Isle of Patmos, he saw an image of Jesus Christ with a double-edged sword emerging from His mouth (Rev. 1:16). What does this tell us about the power of the Word of God to judge?

6. Do you read the Bible merely out of habit or do you expect the Lord to convict you of sin and bring you to repentance through His Word? Give examples of when God's Word has cut to your heart and convicted you of sin in your life.

7. Read Psalm 139. Pay attention to the verbs in this passage. What do these words reveal about the abilities and power of God? What feeling does this knowledge leave with you?

8. How would you define "repent"? Compare Ezekiel 33:11 and Matthew 12:41. Who are the recipients of each command to repent? What does this suggest about God's ultimate plan of redemption?

9. Think of some well-known characters of the Bible. How many people can you identify who experienced a genuine repentance, or turning from sin?

CHAPTER 12

UNDERSTANDING
Understanding How God Speaks

CONTEXT

Gen. 30:1-6 *"When Rachel saw that she was not bearing Jacob any children, she envied her sister. 'Give me sons, or I will die!' she said to Jacob. Jacob became angry with Rachel and said, 'Am I in God's place, who has withheld children from you?' Then she said, 'Here is my slave Bilhah. Go sleep with her, and she'll bear children for me so that through her I too can build a family.' So Rachel gave her slave Bilhah to Jacob as a wife, and he slept with her. Bilhah conceived and bore Jacob a son. Rachel said, 'God has vindicated me; yes, He has heard me and given me a son,' and she named him Dan.*

I HAVE THE RESPONSIBILITY OF taking my kiddos to their GiGi's house every morning before heading off to work. Every morning before leaving, I give each one of them a good-bye kiss. Recently Makenna, my two-year-old daughter, has decided on some days that she doesn't want her daddy's good-bye kiss. So when I go to say my good-byes, she'll scream "No kisses!" and bury her face.

After a couple of days of this, I had an ingenious idea. Since she loves chocolate, and since GiGi always keeps a container stocked with Hersey's Kisses, I pulled one of the bite-sized chocolates out, held it up, and simply asked, "Would you like a kiss?"

Her immediate response was "Yes!" As she went to grab the chocolate kiss from my hand, I quickly planted a smooch on her cheek. I got my good-bye kiss, and she got her chocolate. Everyone walked away happy. To put it another way, we could say: "Both are happy that Makenna received a kiss from her daddy."

Look at that sentence. Both me and my daughter would be able to say that it accurately describes the situation, yet we mean different things. I am happy because I got to show my daughter affection before parting for the day. She is happy because she gets to eat a bit of chocolate before breakfast. The point is that we have to know more information before we can understand the fullness of that simple statement.

Reading the Bible require this same type of commitment. There are many things in the Bible that, if pulled apart from the rest of the book, would be very confusing or troubling. A prime example is the passage above. If we don't understand the historical situation, the type of writing, and the ultimate point of the passage, we will have huge questions surrounding the Bible. In other words, for us to truly understand and apply the Bible to our lives, we must understand the context in which passages are written.

PAUSE AND REFLECT

▷ **What is context?**

▷ **Why is it important to understand the context of a passage of Scripture?**

▷ **What can happen if we try to apply Scripture without understanding the context?**

GENRE

Prov. 22:6 *"Teach a youth about the way he should go; even when he is old he will not depart from it."* **Prov. 26:4-5** *"Don't answer a fool according to his foolishness or you'll be like him yourself. Answer a fool according to his foolishness or he'll become wise in his own eyes."* **Also read Joel 2:17-21, and Acts 2:14-21.**

NETFLIX STREAMING IS AWESOME. WITH just a few clicks, you can instantly watch any number of television shows or movies. On of the most time consuming elements of the entire process is deciding what to watch.

To help users in the endeavor, Netflix has all of their content categorized by genre. So if you're hanging out with a couple of buddies and want a good laugh, you simply click over to the comedy section and pick from those options. Interested in learning about real-world events and people? Browse the documentary section. Whatever the mood or occasion, you can search through the genre to find your perfect programming.

In addition, selecting a program using this method helps set the mood and tone. If you're going to watch a slap-stick comedy, you probably don't have to pay as close of attention to the small things going on than if you were watching a mystery. The point is, knowing the genre of the program not only helps you choose what you want to watch, but also sets the tone for how you will watch.

This latter statement applies to Bible study as well. Knowing the genre of a passage of Scripture helps set the tone of what to expect, and how to understand, that text. For example, we must understand the book of Proverbs to be a part of what's called 'wisdom literature.' Proverbs 22:6, for instance, says that if parents will teach their children the way they should go, they will remain faithful as they age. Generally speaking, this is the case. More times than not, if a parent instills strong biblical principles in his or her children, they will have a much better chance of being a faithful Christian as they grow older. But that is not always the case. You probably know people who have strong Christian parents but are far away from Christ personally.

If we didn't understand the genre of 'wisdom literature,' we may think that Bible is wrong in these cases. Understanding exactly what this genre is and what it entails, however, let's us learn and teach these types of passages correctly.

PAUSE AND REFLECT

▷ **What is a genre?**

▷ **Why is it important to know the genre of the Scripture passages we study?**

▷ **How can the a passage's genre affect our interpretation of it?**

PURPOSE

Gal. 1:1-7 *"Paul, an apostle—not from men or by man, but by Jesus Christ and God the Father who raised Him from the dead—and all the brothers who are with me: To the churches of Galatia. Grace to you and peace from God the Father and our Lord Jesus Christ, who gave Himself for our sins to rescue us from this present evil age, according to the will of our God and Father. To whom be the glory forever and ever. Amen. I am amazed that you are so quickly turning away from Him who called you by the grace of Christ and are turning to a different gospel—not that there is another gospel, but there are some who are troubling you and want to change the good news about the Messiah."*

I RECENTLY PURCHASED A HOME gym. It's one of those large machines that allow you to do over 30 different exercises in a variety of positions. I ordered the machine on the internet, and was shocked when it arrived at my house. The entire contraption was stuffed into a box that less than 8 inches tall! As I opened the box up, I started to see how it was in fact possible. Before starting the construction process, I sought out the owner's manual.

In the brief manual, I was provided detailed instructions for putting the machine together, a helpful guide for the various exercises that could be performed on the machine, and a few training tips. This was a very helpful guide. But it was only helpful because I had that particular machine.

If I were to approach you and give you this manual, you'd have absolutely no use for it. The entire manual is written for the purpose of showing someone how to set up and use the equipment. If they do not have the equipment, the manual would do no good.

Just as the instruction manual had a very specific purpose, much of the Bible does as well. If we do not understand the purpose of a specific text of Scripture, we may miss it's ultimate point

For example, look at this passage from Galatians. Verse 2 clearly states that this letter was written to the churches of Galatia. Why did Paul choose to write this particular letter to those churches? We see that answer a bit further in verses 6 and 7. He explicitly says that there are some in the church of Galatia that wanted "to change the gospel of Christ." The purpose of this letter, then, is to help the churches of Galatia understand the true gospel and protect them from false doctrines. If we didn't have this first section to help us see the purpose of the letter, we'd miss out on much of its rich teaching.

PAUSE AND REFLECT

▷ Why is it important to understand the writer's purpose of a particular passage of Scripture?

▷ How does knowing a passage's purpose help us understand the ultimate meaning of a passage?

▷ How can we figure out a passage's purpose?

UNDERSTANDING HOW GOD SPEAKS

To rightly understand God's Word, we need to understand How god communicated.

WHAT WOULD YOU THINK if I told you that you were an alien? Not the scaly green kind with big foreheads but the biblical kind. The kind Peter talked about when he reminded the Christians living in Asia Minor that they were "strangers and temporary residents" (1 Pet. 2:11).

To be an alien, in the biblical sense, is to belong to another land. It's the idea that our ultimate citizenship belongs to another Kingdom, to another King. The Bible consistently teaches that Christians are a sojourning society, traveling from one world to the next.

God has given His Word to His traveling pilgrims—the Holy Scripture. In it we discover how to travel, where to travel, and the ways in which we can bring others along on the journey. But the Scriptures must be interpreted correctly in order for it to make sense. Written in the contexts of numerous empires and eras, the biblical writers differed greatly from one another. There were humble shepherds like David and wise sages like Solomon, simple fishermen like Peter and educated scholars like Paul.

Failing to understand each writer and the *context*, *genre*, and *purpose* of such writings can lead not only to a skewed understanding of Scripture but also to unnecessary heartache, confusion, and misdirection.

In this chapter, we'll explore four genres of Scripture that will help us interpret God's Word responsibly: historical narrative, wisdom literature, prophecy, and letters. By focusing on these four styles of writing, we can acquire several principles and guidelines in order to understand not only a particular passage of Scripture but also how that passage fits into the overarching narrative of God's redeeming plans.

▶ INTERPRETING HISTORICAL NARRATIVE (GEN. 30:1-6)

¹ When Rachel saw that she was not bearing Jacob any children, she envied her sister. "Give me sons, or I will die!" she said to Jacob. ² Jacob became angry with Rachel and said, "Am I in God's place, who has withheld children from you?"
³ Then she said, "Here is my slave Bilhah. Go sleep with her, and she'll bear

children for me so that through her I too can build a family." ⁴ So Rachel gave her slave Bilhah to Jacob as a wife, and he slept with her. ⁵ Bilhah conceived and bore Jacob a son. ⁶ Rachel said, "God has vindicated me; yes, He has heard me and given me a son," and she named him Dan.

A Sunday School teacher in Nebraska once asked a group of fourth-graders, "What is the hardest commandment for you to keep?" One replied, "Thou shalt not commit adultery." When asked what adultery meant, he explained, "It means 'Do not talk back to adults.'"

Misunderstanding the words of Scripture is not merely a fourth-grade problem. Adults can fail to understand them too. And in some cases, the outcome of this misunderstanding can be heartbreaking.

In January 2011, 28-year-old John Joe Thomas read Leviticus 20:13 and then acted on his reading by stoning to death a 70-year-old man. Charged with first-degree murder, Thomas claimed that his reading of the Old Testament compelled him to do it.[3]

Stories like these are extreme, but they serve to remind us of the importance of rightly interpreting God's Word. In the passage above, we read an R-rated narrative in which Jacob's wife Rachel cannot become pregnant. So she tells her husband to commit adultery with Bilhah, her slave. Jacob obeys his wife and sleeps with Bilhah, who becomes pregnant with two sons, Dan and Naphtali.

For us to interpret this passage correctly, we need to understand the genre of historical narrative. Approximately 60 percent of the Bible is historical narrative. Sidney Greidanus says historical narrative is the "central, foundational, and all-encompassing genre of the Bible."[4] The purpose of historical narrative literature is simply to narrate, to tell a story.

Some of these stories contain acts of great faith, like that of Abraham who left his home in Ur to travel as a pilgrim and alien to a foreign land. Other stories contain acts of great heroism, like Samson, who picked up the jawbone of a donkey and slayed one thousand Philistines.

The Bible contains stories of encouragement and depression, sorrows and celebrations. The characters are many. There is Solomon in his sanctuary and Daniel in his den, Jonah in his whale and Paul in his prison. The plots are unpredictable—a slave who became powerful in Egypt; a shepherd who became king of Israel. Some of these stories reflect the faithfulness of God's people, while others reflect the consequences of neglecting to obey God.

Rachel's story reflects the disobedience of neglecting God's standard. Rachel "envied her sister" because of her sons. Just as Eve tempted Adam and Adam succumbed to her temptation, so Rachel sparked in Jacob's mind a sin that caused them both to stray from God's holy standard. This story was included in the canon of

Scripture to describe the events of Jacob's life, not to encourage us to follow in his sin.

It is vitally important to understand the context of a historical narrative. There are three primary kinds of context. *Immediate context*—the words, phrases, sentences, and paragraphs immediately surrounding the biblical text. *Remote context*—the chapters and sections surrounding the biblical text. And *historical context*—the historical setting in which the biblical text was written. Each of these contexts is important in determining how to interpret a particular passage in Scripture.

▶ INTERPRETING WISDOM LITERATURE (PROV. 22:6; 26:4-5)

⁶ Teach a youth about the way he should go; even when he is old he will not depart from it.

⁴ Don't answer a fool according to his foolishness or you'll be like him yourself.
⁵ Answer a fool according to his foolishness or he'll become wise in his own eyes.

Interpreting the proverbs as promises is a critical mistake that can fuel legalism, moralism, and disillusionment. Once again, we see the importance of knowing how to interpret the different genres of Scripture and the heartache that comes from a misguided interpretation.

The Book of Proverbs is a collection of wise sayings that is categorized under the umbrella of wisdom literature. Unlike the genre of historical narrative that purposes to tell a story, wisdom literature provides general truths about living in a way that honors God.

A proverb is a pithy and persuasive statement or series of statements that has been proven true by experience. However, proverbs are not proven true in every case. For instance, Proverbs 3:1-3 says that if you obey the commandments in Scripture, "they will bring you many days, a full life." This doesn't mean that all Christians who obey God's commandments will live into their late 70s and 80s. Instead, it means that if you live a life of discipline (1:2), avoid falling into sexual promiscuity (2:16-19), maintain character and integrity in your relationships (3:29-30), and guard your lips from lies (4:24), then it is generally true that the pitfalls that come from sinful actions will escape you.

Not always though. Sometimes obeying God's commandments can directly lead to premature death. Take Stephen, for instance. After being faithful to Christ's instructions to preach the gospel to all nations (Mark 16:15), Stephen boldly proclaimed God's truth and was stoned to death (Acts 7:54-60). Proverbs are general truths. We need to interpret them in that way.

Likewise, we cannot pull one proverb out of context and apply it universally. The two proverbs in Proverbs 26:4-5 appear to contradict one another until you realize that the author is referring to different circumstances. Sometimes it's best to speak to the fool; other times it's best to stay silent.

Like the Book of Proverbs, the other books of wisdom literature (Job, Psalms, Song of Songs, and Ecclesiastes) must be interpreted according to their individual purposes. Whereas Job sheds light on the proper relationship between God and people, Psalms contains a variety of purposes: lament and petition, thanksgiving and praise, exaltation of the king, and expressions of trust. These purposes must be interpreted according to each individual category within the Psalms.

What about Ecclesiastes? The purpose of Ecclesiastes is to show us by negative example how best to behave. For instance, when the author says, "Everything is futile" (Eccl. 1:2), we must interpret this in light of other Scripture verses that explain the true meaning and ultimate value of living a godly life (Rom. 12:2; 15:14; Eph. 5:8; 2 Pet. 1:3-11).

Here's the bottom line: misinterpreting wisdom literature can point us in the wrong direction, away from a life that honors and glorifies God. Jill never returned to the faith she was raised to observe…at least not yet. But who knows? Like the prodigal son who "came to his senses," Proverbs 22:6 might just prove to be true in Jill's case after all.

▶ **INTERPRETING PROPHECY (JOEL 2:28-32)**

28After this I will pour out My Spirit on all humanity; then your sons and your daughters will prophesy, your old men will have dreams, and your young men will see visions. 29I will even pour out My Spirit on the male and female slaves in those days. 30I will display wonders in the heavens and on the earth: blood, fire, and columns of smoke. 31The sun will be turned to darkness and the moon to blood before the great and awe-inspiring Day of the LORD comes. 32Then everyone who calls on the name of Yahweh will be saved, for there will be an escape for those on Mount Zion and in Jerusalem, as the LORD promised, among the survivors the LORD calls.

On May 21, 2011, the followers of "prophet" Harold Camping turned their eyes to the skies in anticipation of the Second Coming of Jesus. These individuals had sold possessions, listed houses on the market, given large sums of money to the doomsday campaign, and even found suitable homes for beloved pets. Jesus was coming back, they believed. They had to be ready. On May 22, the "prophet" turned out to be false. But how? In his Bible, Camping had read Genesis 7:4, "Seven days from now I will make it rain on the earth," and also 2 Peter 3:8, "With the Lord one day is like a thousand years, and a thousand years like one day." From these two passages he concluded that Christ's return would occur exactly 7,000 years after Noah's flood (4990 b.c.). All that was left to do was the math. 2011 + 4990 − 1 (there is no year between 1 b.c. and a.d. 1) = 7,000. Right? Wrong. Jesus did not return on May 22, and the false prophet went into hiding.

Of all the genres of Scripture, prophecy is one of the most difficult to understand, interpret, and apply to our lives. The first step in correctly interpreting prophetic literature is to seek to understand what the author sought to communicate to his original audience.

Sometime between 900 b.c. and 400 b.c., a massive swarm of locusts infiltrated Judah. We don't know how widespread this plague was, but in 1889, it was reported that one swarm of locusts crossed the Red Sea and covered a staggering 2,000 square miles.[8] The locusts wreaked havoc on Judah's vegetation and livestock. "Powerful and without number" (Joel 1:6), these creatures destroyed fields, devastated grapevines, stripped bark from trees, withered orchards, and blocked out the rays of the sun over the land.

Against the backdrop of this devastating plague, Joel urged God's people to repent by tearing not just their clothes but also their hearts (2:13). "Who knows?" Joel pondered, "[God] may turn and relent and leave a blessing behind Him" (v. 14). And that's exactly what happened. After the people of God wept, mourned, and fasted for their nation, God restored their land and "spared His people" (v. 18).

▶ FORETELLERS AND FORTHTELLERS

By calling the nation to repent of its sin, Joel was a *forthteller*, that is, he put forth God's truth to his own generation. But Joel and other prophets were also *foretellers* who spoke to the fulfillment of future events. In our passage today, Joel spoke not only to the immediate outpouring of God's blessing but also to a future outpouring of God's Spirit. "I will pour out My Spirit on all humanity; then your sons and your daughters will prophesy, your old men will have dreams, and your young men will see visions" (Joel 2:28). This prophecy came true hundreds of years later during the ministry of the apostle Peter (see Acts 2:14-21).

But Joel's prophecy did not end with Peter at Pentecost. In fact, Joel 2:30-32 has yet to be fulfilled, even in our lifetime. Revelation 6:12 and 8:7 suggest that these events, prophesied thousands of years ago, are still on the horizon.

▶ INTERPRETING LETTERS (GAL. 1:1-7)

¹ Paul, an apostle—not from men or by man, but by Jesus Christ and God the Father who raised Him from the dead— ² and all the brothers who are with me:
To the churches of Galatia.

³ Grace to you and peace from God the Father and our Lord Jesus Christ, ⁴ who gave Himself for our sins to rescue us from this present evil age, according to the will of our God and Father. ⁵ To whom be the glory forever and ever. Amen.

⁶ I am amazed that you are so quickly turning away from Him who called you by the grace of Christ and are turning to a different gospel— ⁷ not that there is another gospel, but there are some who are troubling you and want to change the good news about the Messiah."

Picture yourself driving to work, not necessarily paying attention to your speed. Suddenly you see in your rearview mirror the dreaded flash of red and blue. Most of us have been in that situation. In fact, over 34 million tickets are issued each year (nearly 100,000 daily). Failure to abide by these laws contributes to over 10,000 deaths every year.[10]

The letters (also called epistles) constitute a major section in the New Testament. Similar to an e-mail that you might write to a friend or a group of friends, each letter has a particular author and audience.

Take Galatians, for instance, written by Paul to the churches in Galatia around A.D. 50. It's a short letter, only six chapters long. It includes an introduction, a description of Paul's apostleship, a treatise on the relationship between grace and the law, an appeal, a thesis on what it means to be free in Jesus Christ, and a conclusion. Its primary purpose is to encourage Christians to return to the gospel that they have abandoned.

The Galatians didn't understand how to obey the law—not the traffic law but the law of God. "I am amazed that you are so quickly turning away from Him who called you by the grace of Christ and are turning to a different gospel," wrote Paul (1:6). That's why Paul spent so many words explaining the importance of the law and how the law must be obeyed in relationship to the gospel of grace.

In essence, the churches in Galatia thought that simply obeying the law was enough. By going the speed limit, so to speak, they thought God would be honored with their lives and save them. What they didn't understand is that God desires more than just outward obedience; He desires inward transformation that *results* in outward obedience.

After the author, audience, and structure of an epistle are established, we can then proceed to discover its meaning for our lives. But we must do so carefully, for some teachings in the Bible are culturally mandated to specific audiences.

For instance, in 1 Corinthians 11:6, Paul writes, "If a woman's head is not covered, her hair should be cut off." Is the application of this text to mean that the women in our churches should wear hats to church every week or else shave their heads? Not necessarily. The church in Corinth would have understood completely that Paul was giving this instruction because prostitutes in the city of Corinth would identify themselves by displaying their long hair in public. Paul wanted to make it very clear that Christian women must act differently than the world. So the application of this passage lies in the principle behind what Paul was saying—modesty—not hair length and accessories.

Determining which texts are culturally mandated can be challenging, and Bible-loving people disagree often. Nevertheless, using this guide to escort us through Scripture as a way to understand the epistles will give greater clarity about how to apply God's Word to your life.

▶ CONCLUSION

Two men were traveling by foot from Jerusalem to Emmaus. They were talking about the crucifixion of Jesus when suddenly Jesus joined them on their journey. As they walked, the conversation turned to Scripture. "Then beginning with Moses and all the Prophets, He interpreted for them the things concerning Himself in all the Scriptures" (Luke 24:27). In essence, the great Teacher gave them a proper understanding of how God speaks through His Word.

God's people were never meant to walk in this world alone. We are pilgrims who require God's guidance. When it comes to interpreting the Word of God, Jesus does not leave us to ourselves. He does not want us to experience the unnecessary heartache and confusion that come from misinterpreting His words. That's why He joins us in our pilgrimages—He escorts us to eternity—and shows us how to correctly read the Scripture. And He delights in our seeing how everything (even the strange stories of the Old Testament) is ultimately designed to lead us to Him.

If you and I allow Christ to lead us through the genres of Scripture, to guide us through the landscape of hermeneutics, then we can be confident that God will go before us, behind us, and beside us. "Remember," Jesus said, "I am with you always, to the end of the age" (Matt. 28:20).

QUESTIONS

1. What would be some improper interpretations or applications of this passage? Taken out of context, what does this passage seem to allow?

2. What is the immediate, remote, and historical context of Genesis 30:1-6? How does knowing the context help us interpret and apply the individual story? When in your life has something you have said been taken out of context and what were the results? How was what you said misinterpreted?

3. What are some other proverbs that are generally true and yet not applicable to every circumstance? What are some proverbs we live by culturally that aren't from the Bible even though some attribute them to the Bible? What is the difference in sound worldly common sense and biblical wisdom?

4. Read Deuteronomy 13:1-5 and 18:21-22. According to these passages, what distinguishes a true prophet from a false prophet? When you hear someone in the media claim to know when Christ will return, what are your thoughts? Why do you feel the way you do?

5. What are some ways in which ancient letters are different than the letters we write today? What are some similarities? How does knowledge of ancient letter-writing help us understand the New Testament letters?

6. How might something you say to one particular friend differ from the way you would tell the same info to another person? What if you were describing a friends party you went to? How would your description differ if you were telling an adult, a friend, or a teacher?

7. What can you do to remember these truths as you read God's Word to help you properly interpret what is being said? Do you understand now why beginning with prayer and asking God to guide is such an important part of studying the Bible?

CHAPTER 13
LISTENING TOGETHER
Listening Together to the Voice of God

REVERENCE OF GOD'S WORD

Neh. 8:4-6 *Ezra the scribe stood on a high wooden platform made for this purpose. Mattithiah, Shema, Anaiah, Uriah, Hilkiah, and Maaseiah stood beside him on his right; to his left were Pedaiah, Mishael, Malchijah, Hashum, Hash-baddanah, Zechariah, and Meshullam. Ezra opened the book in full view of all the people, since he was elevated above everyone. As he opened it, all the people stood up." Ezra praised the Lord, the great God, and with their hands uplifted all the people said, "Amen, Amen!" Then they bowed down and worshiped the Lord with their faces to the ground. "*

WHY DO WE CALL OUR teacher, 'Mr. Smith' instead of 'John'?

Why do we answer our parents with a 'yes ma'am' or 'yes sir' instead of 'yup.'?

Why do we refer to the president as 'President Washington,' instead of 'George' or even 'Mr. Washington.'?

All of these titles are signs of respect in the American culture. There are many things we do in our lives that have no real function other than demonstrating respect. Yet, our culture values these things very highly.

Just as we have great respect for certain individuals, and address them accordingly, we find in the book of Nehemiah that the people of God had a great respect for God's Word. The word 'reverence' means to have a deep or great respect. So, essentially the Israelites highly revered, or had reverence for, God's Word.

This reverence manifested in several ways. We see that a great assembly of people gathered to hear the reading of God's Word (v.2). The Word was read aloud and all the people 'listened attentively' (v.3). When the Word was read, the people stood up (v.5), and immediately thereafter they bowed down and worshiped with their faces to the ground (v.6).

Why did the Israelites do these various things as God's Word was being read? These things were done out of deep reverence. They understood that what was being read was the very Word of God, and they treated it with extreme devotion.

PAUSE AND REFLECT

▷ **Do you revere God's Word? Why or why not?**

▷ **Why is it important to have a reverence for God's Word?**

▷ **How can you develop and display your reverence for God's Word?**

PREPARATION TO RECEIVE GOD'S WORD

Neh. 8:7-12 *"Jeshua, Bani, Sherebiah, Jamin, Akkub, Shabbethai, Hodiah, Maaseiah, Kelita, Azariah, Jozabad, Hanan, and Pelaiah, who were Levites, explained the law to the people as they stood in their places. They read out of the book of the law of God, translating and giving the meaning so that the people could understand what was read. Nehemiah the governor, Ezra the priest and scribe, and the Levites who were instructing the people said to all of them, "This day is holy to the Lord your God. Do not mourn or weep." For all the people were weeping as they heard the words of the law. Then he said to them, "Go and eat what is rich, drink what is sweet, and send portions to those who have nothing prepared, since today is holy to our Lord. Do not grieve, because the joy of the Lord is your stronghold." And the Levites quieted all the people, saying, "Be still, since today is holy. Do not grieve." Then all the people began to eat and drink, send portions, and have a great celebration, because they had understood the words that were explained to them."*

IN TODAY'S WORLD, WHERE NUTRITION and fitness have become increasingly chic, completing a marathon has become an ultimate goal for many. This 26.2 mile endurance run promises a great sense of accomplishment for those who complete it. It should go without saying, however, that completing a marathon is no easy task. A great deal of training is required to even complete a marathon, much less compete with other racers. For those already in reasonably good shape, it may take up to half a year of daily training in order to fully prepare the body and mind for the race. For those out of shape, even more.

Interestingly, this ought to be the same way we approach God's Word. We should not expect to flippantly open the Bible, turn to a random verse, read it, and truly encounter the living God. Look at the care and devotion to God's Word in our text. In this passage, we see that the people explained, read, translated, and gave a clear meaning of the text to those in need of God's Word. Then, they proceeded to tell the people to eat, cease their grieving, and begin rejoicing in the Lord. And the people did, "because they had understood the words that were explained to them. (Neh. 8:12)" Look at all of the work that went into understanding the Scriptures. Understanding came after a long process of preparation and training for receiving God's Word. If we truly want to encounter the power of God's Word, we must be willing to prepare for receiving God's Word.

PAUSE AND REFLECT

▷ **What does it mean to prepare to receive God's Word?**

▷ **Practically speaking, how would one go about preparing to receive God's Word?**

▷ **Why is it important that you prepare to receive God's Word personally?**

POWER OF GOD'S WORD

Acts 2:42 *"And they devoted themselves to the apostles' teaching, to the fellowship, to the breaking of bread, and to the prayers."*

WHERE I LIVE (NORTH TEXAS), we don't get much snow and ice, but when we do get the wintry precipitation, it can be a recipe for disaster. This is especially so at my parent's house, which is in a fairly rural setting. This means that when ice starts to cause problems with the power lines, my parents are some of the last to get their electricity restored. During one particular cold snap my senior year of high school, our family went without power for about 3 days.

Not wanting to get caught in a situation like this again, my dad has now purchased a generator for those rare winter storms. Now when power lines go down, a simple starting of the generator provides energy to run the lights, heat, and TV (the big 3, in my opinion), until the electric company can get everything back and running.

Think about this for a minute. Every single power button and light switch in the house can instantly be restored by simply turning on the generator. This source of energy allows everything else to function. Without it, we are cold, dark, and bored. With it we have light, heat, and excitement. That single generator provides all of those things.

Notice here in Acts how God's Word serves a similar impact on true Christian community. By being devoted to the Apostles' teaching (God's Word), they by extension fellowshipped together, broke bread together, and prayed together. That is, God's Word essentially served as the life source for the Christian community. The power of God's Word enabled those early believers to live their lives in close relationships with each other, constantly seeking ways to worship and obey Christ.

We need this same type of community today. We often gather around sporting events and other social happenings, but how often do we gather around God's Word? We are quite good at fellowship, but we need to examine our reasons for fellowship.

PAUSE AND REFLECT

▷ Why is God's Word so powerful?

▷ How does the power of God's Word affect your life?

▷ How can you harness the power of God's Word to impact the community you have with other people?

LISTENING TOGETHER FOR THE VOICE OF GOD

Biblical community exists when God's Word is proclaimed and revered, repentance and accountability are present, and disciples are being made.

IT ALL STARTED when my wife and her family rented a beach house for a few weeks in Florida. My plan was simple: I was going to stay on the round plastic floatie in the ocean for just a few minutes. After about an hour or so, the soothing rocking of the waves had drifted me to sleep…*and* a hundred yards away from shore. It was the first moment in my life when I have ever felt truly alone. After a few terrifying seconds, I managed to glimpse a small sliver of land hovering on the horizon. Minutes later, I was safe on shore.

Have you ever felt alone? Maybe you've never fallen asleep in the middle of the ocean, but all of us have experienced feelings of loneliness at one time or another. Perhaps you've just moved to a new community and you haven't made any friends yet. Maybe you switched schools and aren't fitting in yet. None of us are immune to feelings of isolation.

Unlike us, God is never alone. From all eternity, He has existed in three Persons—the Father, the Son, and the Holy Spirit. We call this truth the "Trinity." Make no mistake. God is a personal God, and He has emotions. He experiences regret (Gen. 6:6), anger (Ps. 106:40), jealousy (Ex. 20:5), love (1 John 4:8), and so forth. But not loneliness. And that's why after Christ rose from the dead, He made sure His disciples would never be alone.

You and I were not made to be alone. We were made for life *together*. Biblical fellowship with other Christians is centered on God's Word. We proclaim God's Word, revere God's Word, and respond to God's Word in repentance. This chapter, as we examine a Word-based understanding of biblical community in Nehemiah 8 and Acts 2, we will see that God designed His Word to be the bedrock of our fellowship and the impetus for our evangelism.

Biblical Community Exists When...

▶ GOD'S WORD IS PROCLAIMED (NEH. 8:1-2).

¹all the people gathered together at the square in front of the Water Gate. They asked Ezra the scribe to bring the book of the law of Moses that the LORD had given

Israel. ²On the first day of the seventh month, Ezra the priest brought the law before the assembly of men, women, and all who could listen with understanding.

According to statistics, the average attention span of an adult is no more than 20 minutes. Due to the rise of fast-paced Internet browsing, television commercials, and other forms of instant gratification media, the number might actually be much lower.

In Nehemiah 8, the Israelites "listened attentively" to the Book of the Law (the Pentateuch) for about six hours, from morning to noon. Just imagine it. What if your church decided to meet for six hours this Sunday? To us, that might seem like a long time to listen to a Scripture reading. But during the days of Nehemiah, the Jewish exiles couldn't get enough of it.

By 586 B.C., the Babylonian Empire had conquered the Southern Kingdom of Judah and had taken God's people into captivity. "By the rivers of Babylon," wrote the psalmist, "there we sat down and wept when we remembered Zion" (Ps. 137:1). It was a difficult season in Israel's history.

But God's discipline had finally come to an end. A new day in the history of the Jews had arrived. When King Cyrus issued an edict allowing the Jews to return to Jerusalem, God's people sought to recover the heritage they had lost in exile. It was time to start rebuilding, to start reforming the walls of the city that had been broken. And central to this reformation was the recovery of Scripture.

Reformation and proclamation always go together. Whenever God starts a genuine reformation in the history of His church, the holy Scripture always takes front and center stage. In fact, one of the banner cries of the sixteenth-century Protestant Reformation was *sola Scriptura* ("by Scripture alone"). This slogan summarized the authority and centrality of the holy Scripture over against the authority of the pope or of tradition. *Sola Scriptura* was the idea that God speaks to His people not through leaders or individuals in power but through the Holy Scripture as it is illuminated by the Holy Spirit.

Nehemiah had a working knowledge of *sola Scriptura* long before Martin Luther nailed his *95 Theses* to a door in 1517. Nehemiah knew that the returning exiles from Babylon could not rebuild their walls and reform their city without hearing a word from the Lord. So when the exiles had settled into their new homes, Ezra, who was a teacher of the law, gathered them together in the square for an appointed time and read to them the ancient words that God had given His people.

We don't know what part of the Law Nehemiah read. Perhaps Ezra reminded these exiles of Joseph and how his brothers had sold him into slavery but "God planned it for good" (Gen. 50:20). It's possible that Ezra opened the scroll of Exodus and recounted the narrative of how God delivered His people from four hundred years of bondage in Egypt and how He had brought them into the promised land after many years of wandering. All of these stories would have grabbed the attention of these Jews, and for many of them, this might have been the first time they had ever heard the Scriptures actually read out loud.

The reading of God's Word reminds us of God's eternal character. It reminds us how we, like the returning exiles, are given the choice either to obey or disobey God. Through the reading of God's Word, we are reminded of our heritage—where we came from and who we are. We are reminded of God's faithfulness to our ancestors and His mighty acts of restoration. But most of all, through the reading of God's Word, we are reminded that God has a master plan, a mission to restore what His people lost—all through the power of the cross of Jesus Christ.

One of the sweetest hopes for Christians is that a day is coming when all forms of captivity will cease—sexual addictions, eating disorders, drug and alcohol abuse, slavery to our own reputations. Death will die, tears will dry up, mourning will turn to morning as God's people bask forever in His glorious presence. But until that day arrives, God has chosen to speak to us through the reading and preaching of His holy Word in the context of biblical community.

▶ GOD'S PEOPLE REVERE GOD'S WORD TOGETHER (NEH. 8:3-6).

³While he was facing the square in front of the Water Gate, he read out of it from daybreak until noon before the men, the women, and those who could understand. All the people listened attentively to the book of the law. ⁴Ezra the scribe stood on a high wooden platform made for this purpose. Mattithiah, Shema, Anaiah, Uriah, Hilkiah, and Maaseiah stood beside him on his right; to his left were Pedaiah, Mishael, Malchijah, Hashum, Hash-baddanah, Zechariah, and Meshullam. ⁵Ezra opened the book in full view of all the people, since he was elevated above everyone. As he opened it, all the people stood up." ⁶Ezra praised the LORD, the great God, and with their hands uplifted all the people said, "Amen, Amen!" Then they bowed down and worshiped the LORD with their faces to the ground.

If you were an ambassador to Burma in 1867, there was a particular way that you had to approach the king. First, you needed to remove your shoes and then disarm yourself of anything resembling a weapon. Next, you would have been required to kneel down and sit on your feet. Failure to abide by these protocols was an offense to the king.[4]

In every culture, the act of kneeling or bowing is virtually always associated with humility. In the East, to kneel in the presence of another is a sign of greeting and respect, much like a handshake or a hug in the West. You and I might not be as familiar with bowing, but during the days of Ezra and Nehemiah, bowing and kneeling were signs of reverence. It was a way to put someone or something above yourself.

That's exactly what the returning Jewish exiles did in Nehemiah 8. They understood that posture mattered. So when the Torah was read, they stood, which was very common in those days (see 9:3). And after the exiles stood for six hours, they all bowed with their faces to the ground to worship God.

Nehemiah 8 teaches us the importance of elevating Scripture in our lives. It shows us that faith cannot be separated from action. Orthodoxy and orthopraxy go hand in hand, that is to say, what we believe cannot be separated from what we practice. That's why theology matters. That's how the head is connected to the heart. True revival—the kind that comes from God—occurs when Scripture is elevated in our lives.

You and I don't have to worry about taking off our shoes in the presence of a Burmese king, but we do have the privilege and opportunity of entering into the presence of the King of kings. And when we do, we'll know, like Moses, that we are standing on holy ground (see Ex. 3).

▶ REPENTANCE AND ACCOUNTABILITY ARE PRESENT (NEH. 8:7-12).

7Jeshua, Bani, Sherebiah, Jamin, Akkub, Shabbethai, Hodiah, Maaseiah, Kelita, Azariah, Jozabad, Hanan, and Pelaiah, who were Levites, explained the law to the people as they stood in their places. 8They read out of the book of the law of God, translating and giving the meaning so that the people could understand what was read. 9Nehemiah the governor, Ezra the priest and scribe, and the Levites who were instructing the people said to all of them, "This day is holy to the LORD your God. Do not mourn or weep." For all the people were weeping as they heard the words of the law. 10Then he said to them, "Go and eat what is rich, drink what is sweet, and send portions to those who have nothing prepared, since today is holy to our Lord. Do not grieve, because the joy of the LORD is your stronghold." 11And the Levites quieted all the people, saying, "Be still, since today is holy. Do not grieve." 12Then all the people began to eat and drink, send portions, and have a great celebration, because they had understood the words that were explained to them.

In Nehemiah 8, we learn that there was a "high wooden platform" from which Ezra read the scroll. We could call this a prototype pulpit. We see that because this platform was constructed prior to the worship event, *people prepared* for this service. Once the Scripture reading got underway, Nehemiah records that the people began raising their hands in the air and shouting, "Amen, Amen!" which affirmed their submission to and agreement with what Ezra was saying.

Last chapter, we examined the role that interpretation plays in understanding the different genres of Scripture. We discussed how, within the context of community, the church reads Scripture in light of the author's intent, the context of the passage, and the type of genre it reflects.

This chapter, we discover that we in the 21st century are not the only community of faith in need of proper interpretation. God's people have always needed assistance in interpreting His Word. In Nehemiah's time, the Jews had forgotten some of their Hebrew heritage because they had lived so long in captivity. So after Ezra read the scroll, the priests and scribes and other leaders standing on the platform began to explain the law to the people.

Today, we might call this a sermon—the explanation or exegesis of a passage. Interestingly enough, in Nehemiah's day there were 13 preachers on stage instead of just one. This suggests there was a system of accountability in the development of their biblical interpretation. No one person was allowed to single-handedly and ultimately decide what God's Word meant for God's people. Instead, a group of leaders and scribes and priests came together to explain the Scriptures.

Translating or explaining the Bible is not just a job for professional translating ministries like Wycliffe Bible Translators. Every pastor, every preacher, every Sunday School teacher, and every disciple-maker also bears this sacred responsibility. In fact, it is the duty of every Christian to ask the questions "How does this Scripture verse relate to my life?" and "How does it relate to my time and culture?" The answers to these questions are not always easy to find. However, we can be confident that every word in the Bible is "profitable for teaching, for rebuking, for correcting, for training in righteousness, so that the man of God may be complete, equipped for every good work" (2 Tim. 3:16-17).

That's what the Jews discovered in Nehemiah 8. The scribes and leaders "read out of the book of the law of God, translating and giving the meaning so that the people could understand what was read." In other words, they explained Scripture. They showed how God's Word was alive and real. They showed that even though the words were written hundreds of years before, the Torah still applied directly to their situation and could deepen their understanding of God and His character.

Whenever Scripture is read, preached, and received, repentance and forgiveness are sure to follow. Godly repentance carries with it the idea of turning—turning away from sin, away from lustful and evil desires, and turning to face God. Notice in the passage how quickly the mood changes. First, the people express their brokenness and grief over their sin. But then the Word heals and comforts, leading to great celebration.

True repentance is borne out of a broken heart, but it results in the joy of basking in God's forgiveness.

▶ DISCIPLES ARE BEING MADE (ACTS 2:42).

⁴²And they devoted themselves to the apostles' teaching, to the fellowship, to the breaking of bread, and to the prayers.

During the medieval era in Europe, it was common for a member of a family to draw water from a well or spring near the village. Back in those days, there were no water filters or other purification systems. There were no grocery stores where you could pop in and purchase a liter of Evian or Fiji water. Communities could not function without water, so drawing water from the well was one of the most important jobs in the village. Failure to find a fresh source of drinkable water often resulted in illness.

The Protestant Reformers understood the importance of Scripture in the context of community. They used the phrase *ad fontes* ("to the fountains") to say, "Hey, we don't need popes or religious leaders drawing water for us. We can draw it for ourselves!" And that's exactly what they did. To fulfill that sentiment, Martin Luther translated the Bible into the language of the German people so that everyone could read God's Word.

Long after Ezra read the scroll to the returning exiles of Jerusalem, another event would take place in that city—Pentecost. After Jesus ascended into heaven, the apostle Peter "stood up with the Eleven, raised his voice," and then preached a sermon to a large multitude of Jews from every nation (Acts 2:14). In his sermon, Peter incorporated Old Testament verses such as Joel 2:28-32; Psalm 16:8-11; and Psalm 110:1 to help his audience understand the reason that Jesus Christ had died on the cross and been raised from the dead. After the Word of God was proclaimed, the Jews asked Peter and the other apostles, "Brothers, what must we do?" (Acts 2:37). Peter replied, "Repent...and be baptized, each of you, in the name of Jesus Christ for the forgiveness of your sins, and you will receive the gift of the Holy Spirit" (v. 38).

Reverence for the Bible must lead to repentance. There's no sense in revering the Word of God if we are not responding with obedience and faith. Furthermore, Peter understood that without the holy Scriptures, there could be no true Christian community. Peter had been there to hear Jesus say, "Heaven and earth will pass away, but My words will never pass away" (Luke 21:33). Peter watched the Pharisees misquote and twist Scripture when Jesus told them, "You are deceived, because you don't know the Scriptures or the power of God" (Matt. 22:29). Peter knew that the Bible was the fountain—the only uncontaminated source—from which all believers could freely drink. And at Pentecost, approximately three thousand people became followers of Christ that day and were added to the community of faith through baptism.

Scripture-based communities always lead us to reach beyond "the group." Why? Because if our communities take seriously the Word of God, they will act on the commands that Christ gives us in His Word, commands such as "Go, therefore, and make disciples of all nations," (Matt. 28:19). And they will hold on to promises such as "Whoever gives just a cup of cold water to one of these little ones because he is a disciple...He will never lose his reward!" (10:42). The Bible is always pointing us to Christ. And Christ is always pointing us to others. Therefore, if our communities are biblical, they must also be focused on others.

▶ CONCLUSION

There is only one time in the whole Bible that God ever felt really alone. It happened on a Friday. Jesus had celebrated the Passover meal with His disciples. He had endured the torments of Gethsemane, the betrayal of Judas, and the trial before Pontius Pilate. Peter had denied Him. His disciples had abandoned Him. And then, after giving His back to the whip and His hands to the nails, Jesus could not keep His pain silent. He screamed, "My God, my God, why have *You* forsaken Me?" (Matt. 27:46, emphasis added).

Jesus might have understood why His disciples abandoned Him. Judas wanted money. Peter wanted safety. But God? Why would God the Father leave His Son alone at such a critical moment? If Christ had quoted the next part of Psalm 22:1, which must have been in His mind, He would have also screamed, "Why are You so far from my deliverance and from my words of groaning?" In the end, however, Jesus chose to be alone because He wanted you and me to be grafted into the community of faith. He wanted each of us to spend eternity with the God from whom our sins have separated us.

As Christians, we don't have to wait until heaven to experience biblical community. If the holy Scripture is the foundation of our communities and if we choose to obey Christ's commands to spread His gospel and His love in this world, then we can be confident that God will use our communities to be light and truth in a dark and relativistic society. Proclamation of the Word and reverence toward the Word will lead to repentance through the Word.

- What are the foundations for your community with other people?
- What is keeping you from truly connecting on a biblical level with others?
- What areas of your life right now are preventing even fellowship with God through Christ?

QUESTIONS

1. In Nehemiah 8:1-12, the word "people" occurs more than 10 times. What does this say about the purpose of God's people gathered in worship? What are Sunday mornings to you? Have you ever thought about why you gather at church? What reasons would you list as why you meet together at church?

2. In what ways can your church demonstrate the Bible's importance in your fellowship and worship? How can gathering and reading God's Word with other believers become a focused effort for you? Does this change your view of attending church?

3. How is our posture toward God evident in the way we live? What posture would you say your life demonstrates? In what ways can we demonstrate our reverence for God's Word? What do the physical actions of standing and bowing communicate about our view of the Bible?

4. Why is it important to prepare your heart before hearing the Word proclaimed? How does initial preparation help us better hear and apply God's Word to our lives? How often do you respond during a sermon? Why does it seems so weird for us to acknowledge affirmation while God's Word is being taught?

5. In what ways can a Christian help "translate" the Bible and make it understandable for non-Christian friends?

6. The apostles' teaching formed the basis for the fellowship of the early church. What can we learn about making disciples from their model? What forms our basis for fellowship today? How can we improve in this area?

7. What are the foundations for your community with other people? What is keeping you from truly connecting on a biblical level with others? What areas of your life right now are preventing even fellowship with God through Christ?

We demonstrate our trust in God's Word when we know it, when we believe it, and when we proclaim it boldly.

When we submit our lives to God we accept His truths, He changes our heart, and He continues to refine us.

To rightly understand God's Word, we need to understand How god communicated.

Biblical community exists when God's Word is proclaimed and revered, repentance and accountability are present, and disciples are being made.

Part 1/Chapter 1

C. S. Lewis, *Mere Christianity* (New York: HarperCollins, 2001), 164.

D. A. Carson, *The God Who Is There* (Grand Rapids: Baker, 2010), 20.

St. Augustine, *Confessions*, trans. Henry Chadwick (Oxford: Oxford University Press, 1991), X.xxvii (38), quoted in *Inquiring After God*, ed. Ellen T. Charry (Malden, MA: Blackwell Publishers, 2000), 237.

Helen Keller, *The Story of My Life* (Middlesex: The Echo Library, 2007), 13.

Kyle Snodgrass, *The Gospel in Romans: A Theology of Revelation* (Sheffield: Sheffield Academic Press, 1994), quoted in *The Revelation of God* by Peter Jensen (Downers Grove: InterVarsity Press, 2002), 31.

J. I. Packer, *God Has Spoken: Revelation and the Bible*, 3rd ed. (Grand Rapids: Baker Books, 1993), 50.

Chapter 2

James M. Hamilton Jr., *God's Glory in Salvation Through Judgment: A Biblical Theology* (Wheaton: Crossway, 2010), 53.

Diodore of Tarsus, *Commentary on Psalms 1–51*, trans. Robert C. Hill (Atlanta: Society of Biblical Literature, 2005), 61.

C. S. Lewis, *Mere Christianity* (Westwood, NJ: Barbour and Company, Inc., 1952), 131-32.

Matt Chandler and Jared Wilson, *The Explicit Gospel* (Wheaton: Crossway, 2012), 34.

Chapter 3

W. A. Criswell, *Great Doctrines of the Bible*, vol. 1 (Grand Rapids: Zondervan, 1982), 76-77, quoted in "W. A. Criswell" by Paige Patterson in *Theologians of the Baptist Tradition*, eds. Timothy George and David S. Dockery (Nashville: Broadman & Holman Publishers, 2001), 241.

A. A. Hodge and Benjamin B. Warfield, "Inspiration" in *The Christian Treasury* (Edinburgh: Johnstone, Hunter, & Co., 1881), 267.

Part 2/Chapter 4

Oswald Chambers, "Biblical Ethics" (lecture, Bible Training College and at League of Prayer meetings; talks to soldiers in Egypt, 1947), quoted in *The Quotable Oswald Chambers*, comp. and ed., David McCasland (Grand Rapids: Discovery House Publishers, 2008), 258.

James Montgomery Boice, *Genesis: An Expositional Commentary*, vol. 1 (Grand Rapids: Zondervan, 1985), 135.

A. W. Tozer, *The Pursuit of God* (Radford, VA: Wilder Publications, 2008), 52.

Carson, *The God Who Is There*, 30-31.

Thomas Jefferson, *The Jefferson Bible* (Boston: Beacon Press, 1904), 17.

Carson, *The God Who Is There*, 33.

Michael D. Williams, *Far as the Curse Is Found* (Phillipsburg, NJ: P&R Publishing, 2005), 67.

Arthur Bennett, ed., *The Valley of Vision* (Carlisle, PA: The Banner of Truth Trust, 1975), 145.

John Piper, *Battling Unbelief* (Colorado Springs: Multnomah Ebooks, 2007).

Bennett, ed., *The Valley of Vision*, 181.

Ibid., 17.

Chapter 5

Craig G. Bartholomew and Michael W. Goheen, *The Drama of Scripture* (Grand Rapids: Baker Academic, 2004), 69.

Adrian Rogers, *What Every Christian Ought to Know* (Nashville: Broadman & Holman Publishers, 2005), 71-72.

Stephen J. Lennox, *God's Story Revealed* (Indianapolis: Wesleyan Publishing House, 2009), 100.

Carson, *The God Who Is There*, 62.

Ed Stetzer and Philip Nation, *Compelled by Love* (Birmingham, AL: New Hope, 2008), 57.

Eugene H. Merrill, *HCSB Study Bible* (Nashville: Holman Bible Publishers, 2010), 296, n. 6:4-5; n. 6:6.

Bennett, ed., *The Valley of Vision*, 137.

Carson, *The God Who Is There*, 55.

Chapter 6

John Owen, *Of the Mortification of Sin in Believers*, in *Overcoming Sin & Temptation*, eds. Kelly M. Kapic and Justin Taylor (Wheaton: Crossway, 2006), 50.

Larry Crabb, *Inside Out* (Colorado Springs: NavPress, 2007), 216.

Bennett, ed., *The Valley of Vision*, 37.

Ibid., 148.

Part 3/Chapter 7

Russell D. Moore, *Tempted and Tried* (Wheaton: Crossway, 2011), 36.

Maximus the Confessor, *On the Cosmic Mystery of Jesus Christ*, trans. Paul M. Bowers and Robert Louis Wilkin (Crestwood, NY: St. Vladimir's Seminary Press, 2003), 111, quoted in *Tempted and Tried* by Moore, 41.

Michael E. Wittmer, *Heaven Is a Place on Earth* (Grand Rapids: Zondervan, 2004), 193.

Tim Keller, *The Reason for God* (New York: Dutton, 2008), 177.

Ibid., 180.

Benjamin B. Warfield, *Counterfeit Miracles* (New York: Charles Scribner's Sons, 1918), 3.

Ed Stetzer, *Subversive Kingdom* (Nashville: LifeWay Press, 2011), 27.

John Piper, "Sweeter Than Honey, Better Than Gold," Desiring God [online], 6 January 1991 [cited 21 December 2011]. Available from the Internet: *www.desiringgod.org*.

Chapter 8

Herman Bavinck, *Our Reasonable Faith*, trans. Henry Zylstra (Grand Rapids: Wm. B. Eerdmans Publishing Co., 1956), 116.

Craig L. Blomberg, *Matthew*, vol. 22 in *The New American Commentary* (Nashville: Broadman Press, 1992), 103-104.

Richard Dawkins, *The God Delusion* (New York: First Mariner Books, 2008), 51.

J. I. Packer, *A Quest for Godliness: The Puritan Vision of the Christian Life* (Wheaton: Crossway, 1990), 105.

Chapter 9

Theodoret of Cyrus, *Epistle to the Philippians*, 2:8, in *Commentarius in omnes b. Pauli epistolas* by Theodoret, ed. C. Marriott (Oxford: J. H. Parker, 1852-), 2:53, quoted in *Galatians, Ephesians, Philippians*, ed. Mark J. Edwards, vol. 8 in *Ancient Christian Commentary on Scripture: New Testament* (Downers Grove: InterVarsity Press, 1999), 237.

Stetzer and Nation, *Compelled by Love*, 96.

Charles M. Sheldon, *In His Steps* (Chicago: Advance Publishing Co., 1899), 10, 18.

Part 4/Chapter 10

John R. W. Stott, *Culture and the Bible* (Downers Grove: InterVarsity Press, 1979), 12.

George H. Guthrie, *Read the Bible for Life* (Nashville: B&H Publishing Group, 2011), 29.

John Chrysostom, *Homilies on the Apostles*, 17, in *A Select Library of the Nicene and Post-Nicene Fathers of the Christian Church*, eds. P. Schaff et al., 11:110, quoted in *Acts*, ed. Francis Martin, vol. 5 in *Ancient Christian Commentary on Scripture: New Testament* (Downers Grove: InterVarsity Press, 2006), 87.

Chapter 11

Timothy Keller, *King's Cross* (New York: Dutton, 2011), 121.

Adrian Rogers, *What Every Christian Ought to Know*, 22.

Rahul Bedi, "Indian police pay goes up by a whisker," *The Telegraph* [online], 25 February 2005 [cited 22 November 2011]. Available from the Internet: *www.telegraph.co.uk*.

Lowell Dingus and Mark A. Norell, *Barnum Brown: The Man Who Discovered Tyrannosaurus Rex* (Berkeley: University of California Press, 2010), 90, 119, 311.

C. S. Lewis, *Letters to Malcolm: Chiefly on Prayer* (Orlando: Harcourt, 1992), 22.

Joshua Harris, *Dug Down Deep* (Colorado Springs: Multnomah Books, 2010), 65-66.

Christian George, *Sacred Travels: Recovering the Ancient Practice of Pilgrimage* (Downers Grove: InterVarsity Press, 2006), 113.

Trevin Wax, *Counterfeit Gospels* (Chicago: Moody Publishers, 2011), 55.

Roland H. Bainton, *Here I Stand: A Life of Martin Luther* (Peabody: Hendrickson, 1977), 180.

Sam Storms, "The Ultimate Aim of Theology," Enjoying God Ministries [online], 8 November 2006 [cited 21 December 2011]. Available from the Internet: *www.enjoyinggodministries.com*.

A. W. Tozer, *Man—The Dwelling Place of God* [online e-book; cited 21 December 2011]. Available from the Internet: *worldinvisible.com*.

Chapter 12

Douglas John Hall, *Bound and Free: A Theologian's Journey* (Minneapolis: Augsburg Fortress, 2005), 103.

David S. Dockery, quoted in *Read the Bible for Life*, by George H. Guthrie (Nashville: B&H Publishing Group, 2011), 27.

Action News, "Police: Delco man stoned to death for sex advances" *6abc.com* [online], 18 March 2011 [cited 28 November 2011]. Available from the Internet: *abclocal.go.com/wpvi/index*.

Sidney Greidanus, *The Modern Preacher and the Ancient Text: Interpreting and Preaching Biblical Literature* (Grand Rapids: Wm. B. Eerdmans Publishing Co., 1988), 188.

J. W. Tutt, "Migration and Dispersal of Insects: Orthoptera," in *The Entomologist's Record and Journal of Variation: Volume 11*, ed. J. W. Tutt (New York: Heinsberger, 1899), 15.

Hannah Elliot, "How to Beat a Speeding Ticket," *Forbes.com* [online], 13 April 2009 [cited 29 November 2011]. Available from the Internet: *www.forbes.com*; and U.S. Census Bureau, "Table 1108. Speeding-Related Traffic Fatalities by Road Type, Speed Limit, and State: 2009," *Statistical Abstract of the United States: 2012* [online; cited 29 November 2011]. Available from the Internet: *www.census.gov*.

Martin Luther, *A Commentary on St. Paul's Epistle to the Galatians*, trans. Theodore Graebner (Google eBook: Christian Classics Ethereal Library).

Chapter 13

Martin Luther, "On the Councils and the Church," in *Church and Ministry III*, ed. Eric W. Gritsch, trans. Charles M. Jacobs and Eric W. Gritsch, vol. 41 in *Luther's Works* (Philadelphia: Fortress Press, 1966), 150, quoted in "The Primacy of Preaching" by R. Albert Mohler Jr., in *Feed My Sheep: A Passionate Plea for Preaching* (Lake Mary, FL: Reformation Trust Publishing, 2008), 1.

John Piper, *Finally Alive* (Ross-shire, Scotland: Christian Focus, 2009), 172.

John Nisbet, *Burma Under British Rule—And Before*, vol. 1 (Westminster: Archibald Constable & Co. Ltd., 1901), 30.

Bennett, ed., *The Valley of Vision*, 190.

John Piper, *Let the Nations Be Glad*, 2nd ed. (Grand Rapids: Baker Academic, 2003), 17.

Charles Haddon Spurgeon, *The Metropolitan Tabernacle Pulpit*, vol. XVII (London: Passmore & Alabaster, 1872), 598.

How to Use

Welcome to *The Gospel Project*, a gospel-centered curriculum that dives deep into the things of God, lifts up Jesus, focuses on the grand story of Scripture, and drives participants to be on mission. This short-term resource provides opportunities to study the Bible and to encounter the living Christ. *The Gospel Project* provides you with tools and resources to purposefully study God's Word and to grow in the faith and knowledge of God's Son. And what's more, you can do so in the company of others, encouraging and building up one another.

Here are some things to remember that will help you maximize the usefulness of this resource:

- **Gather a Group.** We grow in the faith best in community with other believers, as we love, encourage, correct, and challenge one another. The life of a disciple of Christ was never meant to be lived alone, in isolation.

- **Pray.** Pray regularly for your group members.

- **Prepare.** This resource includes the Bible study content, three devotionals, and follow-up questions for each chapter. Work through the chapter and devotionals in preparation for each group session. Take notes and record your own questions. Also consider the follow-up questions so you are ready to participate in and add to the discussion, bringing up your own notes and questions where appropriate.

- **Resource Yourself.** Make good use of the additional resources available on the Web at *www.gospelproject.com/additionalresources*. Download a podcast. Read a blog post. Be intentional about learning from others in the faith.

- **Group Time.** Gather together with your group to discuss the chapter and devotional content. Work through the follow-up questions and your own questions. Discuss the material and the implications for the lives of believers and the mission to which we have been called.

- **Overflow.** Remember…*The Gospel Project* is not just a curriculum. WE are the project. The gospel is working on us. Don't let your preparation time be simply about the content. Let the truths of God's Word soak in as you study. Let God work on your heart first, and then pray that He will change the hearts of the other people in your group.

Reading through this section and utilizing the suggested principles and practices will greatly enhance the group experience. First is to accept your limitations. You cannot transform a life. Your group must be devoted to the Bible, the Holy Spirit, and the power of Christian community. In doing so your group will have all the tools necessary to draw closer to God and to each other—and to experience heart transformation.

General Tips

- Prepare for each meeting by reviewing the material, praying for each group member, and asking the Holy Spirit to work through you as you point to Jesus each week.
- Make new attendees feel welcome.
- Think of ways to connect with group members away from group time. The amount of participation you have during your group meetings is directly related to the amount of time you connect with your group members away from the group meeting. Consider sending e-mails, texts, or social networking messages encouraging members in their personal devotion times prior to the session.

Materials Needed

- Bible
- Bible study book
- Pen/pencil

Provide Resources for Guests

An inexpensive way to make first-time guests feel welcome is to provide them a copy of your Bible study book. Estimate how many first-time guests you can expect during the course of your study, and secure that number of books. What about people who have not yet visited your group? You can encourage them to visit by providing a copy of the Bible study book.

A Missional Attitude

A small group seeking to be missional and an international missionary have something in common: an assignment to reach a "people group." What people group is your mission? A group with a missionary mentality thinks like a missionary, asking the question, "What can we do to serve and reach those in our community?" What can you do to help your group have an attitude…a missional attitude?

Great Commission Praying in Your Small Group

When it comes to prayer, every small group operates at one of three levels: class, community, or commission. At the class level, prayer requests tend to be general and safe. At the community level, prayer requests become more personal—and a little less safe. A group sticks its toes in the commission level when it begins to pray about missions in general. It goes deep when it starts praying for people who are far from God right in the offices, schools, stores, teams, recreational centers, and neighborhoods where they do life every day.

Find a Group Project

For most of us, projects tend to find us. But if you are looking for the right project for your group, begin with the group members. List things you would like to do in your community, and describe the needs you would like to meet. What role do you see yourself playing in meeting those needs? Also, scan the community for potential projects. Every community has different needs and opportunities. Here are some places to start: hospitals, local schools, local colleges and universities, public servants, community organizations/events, counseling centers, and support groups.

Name _____ Number _____

E-mail _____

Name _____ Number _____

E-mail _____

Name _____ Number _____

E-mail _____

Name _____ Number _____

E-mail _____

Name _____ Number _____

E-mail _____

Name _____ Number _____

E-mail _____

Name _____ Number _____

E-mail _____

Name _____ Number _____

E-mail _____

Name _____ Number _____

E-mail _____

Name _____ Number _____

E-mail _____

Name _____ Number _____

E-mail _____